SUBTLE ENERGY

························ *and the* ························

WORLD WE EXPERIENCE

RICH RALSTON

BALBOA.
PRESS
A DIVISION OF HAY HOUSE

Balboa Press books may be ordered through booksellers or by contacting:

Balboa Press
A Division of Hay House
1663 Liberty Drive
Bloomington, IN 47403
www.balboapress.com
1 (877) 407-4847

Because of the dynamic nature of the Internet, any web addresses or links contained in this book may have changed since publication and may no longer be valid. The views expressed in this work are solely those of the author and do not necessarily reflect the views of the publisher, and the publisher hereby disclaims any responsibility for them.

The author of this book does not dispense medical advice or prescribe the use of any technique as a form of treatment for physical, emotional, or medical problems without the advice of a physician, either directly or indirectly. The intent of the author is only to offer information of a general nature to help you in your quest for emotional and spiritual well-being. In the event you use any of the information in this book for yourself, which is your constitutional right, the author and the publisher assume no responsibility for your actions.

Any people depicted in stock imagery provided by Thinkstock are models, and such images are being used for illustrative purposes only.
Certain stock imagery © Thinkstock.

Printed in the United States of America.

ISBN: 978-1-4525-8564-2 (sc)
ISBN: 978-1-4525-8566-6 (hc)
ISBN: 978-1-4525-8565-9 (e)

Library of Congress Control Number: 2013919676

Balboa Press rev. date: 11/22/2013

CONTENTS

Part 3

Ego, Self-Evaluation, and Clearing Techniques

Part 4

Meditation, Prayer, and Spirituality

Exercises (by chapter)

Illustrations (by chapter)

PREFACE

My background consists of many Christian-based experiences from which I've gained a strong understanding of the Christian belief system and mode of operation. I realized some time ago that my religious beliefs no longer served me, and I moved on to discover a different perspective and understanding of spirituality. Although I no longer practice Christianity, my personal background and religious experiences that I have shared are intended to help explain my reasons for writing this book.

I spent twenty-five years living a very serious and zealous Christian lifestyle. My involvement covered teaching Bible classes, becoming an ordained evangelist, and preaching the gospel. I also created a missionary network to help indigenous pastors in India and sponsored an orphanage in India.

I believe that most are born with some type of extrasensory ability, commonly referred to as intuition. Intuition is generally influenced by the type of society we live in and parental influence. Children are more open and susceptible to their surroundings and connected energy. To more fully appreciate the human experience and energy we are comprised of, try to feel the emotions you associate with your time spent in or with religion or other aspects of your life, such as education, career, relationships, etc. The purpose of this is to learn about yourself and how your past emotional experiences have influenced you to be the person that you are.

For example, as a small child I was introduced to religion by my aunt, who attended a strict church that believed in the Bible and preached hellfire and damnation. The emotions that swept through me were of fear, guilt, and a sense of dread as the preacher stood in front of the congregation and yelled at everyone. He told us we had to be baptized that day or we would go to hell. I was around six years old at the time, very shy, and sheltered. I had been so sick that my mother, a former schoolteacher, with permission from the school district had homeschooled me that year.

At that point I had had minimal exposure to other people. I was also very sensitive to my own and others' feelings. Were you sensitive to others and your surroundings as a child? Do you still consider yourself sensitive? Your answers to these questions will help you discover more about yourself and how it relates to your spirituality.

The experience was so scary that it kept me away from church until I became an adult. Even though I only visited that church with my aunt three times, I still vividly remember the feelings I experienced as I watched people confess their sins in a white gown, followed by being dunked into water. Somehow this act was supposed to make the person acceptable in the eyes of an almighty God and prevent him or her from being punished in a fiery eternal hell. The feelings I experienced were very alarming, and I knew I didn't want to be part of any sort of similar religious experience. Can you relate to these types of emotions? Even if it doesn't relate to a church experience, it could relate to some other type of life event (i.e., traumatic experience at school, home, work, etc.).

My parents did not want to be involved with church and would not allow me to attend except for the times with my aunt. At some point in our lives, for most of us, we begin to question our existence and desire to find real meaning. We ask questions such as, why am I here? and, what is my purpose?

My spiritual quest began in my twenties. I had several experiences with different religious groups. I spent three years studying lessons with a friend from work, and after many study sessions, the instructor was still unable to answer my questions about the material and did not meet my expectations. I came to a crossroad where I had to decide whether to join them or leave. I chose the latter as there were a few things that really puzzled me.

Women weren't allowed to face the congregation, but instead, they had to face one another and hold a conversation. Why weren't they allowed to look at the congregation? Why would a religious organization have the authority to dictate everyone's beliefs? If heaven was reserved for a certain number of souls already elected by the religious organization, and there was a second opportunity to choose God at the resurrection of the dead, then what was the importance of following a strict religious lifestyle? I decided to leave the strict program and spend my time bass fishing instead. I thought when the resurrection occurred, I would take my chances and opt to serve God at that time.

A couple of years passed, and my wife and I didn't have any children. I was not interested in taking up another religion. Even though I had rejected going to church, I still had a desire to understand God. My wife and I decided we should buy a juicer and clean up our bodies. We purchased a juicer from a pastor's wife. She witnessed to us about Jesus Christ and how we were to be spiritual, rather than religious, by accepting Jesus as our Lord and Savior. We went for it hook, line, and sinker and became "born again."

When we prayed the "sinner's prayer," we both experienced sensations. I felt a significant amount of guilt lift off of me, and my wife felt as though a ball of energy entered her heart. We began attending the pastor's church and stayed for about twenty-five years. I hadn't been in the church very long when I was offered the opportunity to be a trustee. I accepted the opportunity and kept the role for many years. During this time, my wife and I raised three children.

This church relied heavily on music and worshipped God by raising hands, using verbal praises, speaking in tongues (a topic all its own), strict interpretation of the Bible, and sharing gifts of the Spirit, such as prophecy, laying hands on others, tongues, and interpretation of tongues. The congregation displayed a high level of emotion, which was intended to demonstrate that they loved God more than anything else and were happy that God would spare them from his wrath and accept them as his people.

I mentioned that when we are young we are more susceptible to our surroundings. I was born with an exceptional ability to see, feel, and hear things around me. Many people also have this ability but are at a loss to explain or understand it. Spiritual leaders attempted to explain my sensitivity by using the Bible as their source. Since they only used the Bible, their explanations were limited. They also attempted to explain what God, demons, angels, heaven, and hell were.

I became frustrated by these limited explanations and also wondered why the Christian church didn't fulfill what it claimed to be by the writings of the prophets and Jesus. Due to its structure, the church also seemed powerless to change the world. There were also dominating personalities within the church leadership. These factors compelled me to leave. Once I left the church and searched for answers from different sources, the answers to these items became clear. I began to study meditation and the use of subtle energy to explore my sensitivity because I did not want to rely on religion any longer.

During my time spent in India, I experienced life-changing healing and spiritual lessons that revealed how off base I'd been in my religious beliefs. It was truly beneficial to be away from the church and in a foreign country because I was out of my comfort zone. Through dreams and visions, I was shown the love of the Creator. Since then I've been fortunate to meet Frank Jordan, who has over forty years of dowsing and energy work experience. I've studied his books, worked with him, and found my own purpose in these areas as well as my souls' purpose here on earth.

I've developed my healing abilities and have been led to many people with similar backgrounds who felt mistreated, confused, frustrated, and sometimes hopeless as a result of their past religious experiences. I've helped them heal their physical bodies, clear their chakras, clear their minds of harmful thought patterns or beliefs, and clear their energy/emotional blockages to gain and maintain balance in life.

I have acquired much of my understanding about subtle energy from Frank Jordan's books, *Clearing the Way*, and *Clearing the Way to Higher Consciousness Earth-Mind* and *Living with Subtle Energy*. I have also studied *The Light Shall Set You Free* by Dr. Norma Milanovich and Dr. Shirley McCune, which explains the universal laws. I also reference the Holy Bible, *New International Version*. Frank Jordan's books are available for purchase at www.Psi-Tronics.com. The rest of the information in this book has come to me from experience helping others and learning to use my helpers such as Gaia, ancestor spirits, devic spirits, guides, angels, guardians, and ascended masters. While I'm helping someone, I'm learning from my helpers. Nobody has all the answers. It's a constant learning process.

Acknowledgments

Many thanks to Nicole Ralston, with a bachelor of arts in English with writing emphasis, for her editing input and compilation of the book material. I appreciate her ability to condense the content and help me with this accomplishment. She is an inspiration.

Many thanks to Frank Jordan and Joan Hite for their help and assistance with energy work as well as with suggestions for this book.

A grateful acknowledgment to Marcus Eaton for the hours spent drawing the helpful illustrations throughout this book. Marcus is a professional musician with many other artistic talents, and I truly appreciate his contribution.

I am grateful for my wife and family and for their patience as I spent many hours meditating, writing, and discussing with them the various topics throughout the book.

INTRODUCTION

The main purpose of this book is to help you think for yourself. The reason I say this is because I understand that so many people have been influenced by religion, education, careers, relationships, etc., and as a result have been stripped of their personal power.

My goal is to provide an explanation of how energy works and how you connect to it. Additionally, I want to help you regain your power and help you gain control of your emotions (through learning to identify what they are and using the provided techniques to clear them). To help you do this, basic techniques are included, such as how to clear and release harmful energy in your own life. I strongly advise you to practice and utilize the techniques provided until you reach a level of proficiency that enables you to continuously reach clarity and empowerment. The techniques work regardless of your religious beliefs.

Throughout this book, I will endeavor to explain how subtle energy works and how it is related to spirituality. I have the ability to see, feel, and hear energy fields, and I have learned by observation how energy operates in humans and the universe. I am not saying that I know everything—just enough to know that the Prime Creator, the creator of all things in the universe, is much more vast and complex than what we can completely comprehend. We don't need to understand everything at once. We learn in stages as our abilities allow us to digest information and utilize it. Therefore, as you read this book, if a subject is just out of your reach, don't get hung up on it; just move on and grasp what is meaningful for you at this time in your life.

If and/or when you come to the realization that your religious practices or something else in your life is not serving or fulfilling you any longer, the next step is to learn how to recognize emotions that may be blocking you from making beneficial changes and remove them so that you have clarity and confidence to do so. I am not trying to destroy your faith in the fact that there is a Prime Creator. Rather, I want to explain to you what it is and how it works. There is a Prime Creator of the universe, and the book will cover what it is and how it works in conjunction with the world we experience.

Even though this book is basically intended to help religious people understand themselves and the role subtle energy plays in their lives, the questions used below can also be applied to other aspects of our lives, such as education, work, military service, relationships, etc. These areas encapsulate the same emotional experiences. If you'd like to replace the religious aspect with another category, the questions are just as helpful and the answers just as revealing. This concept applies to all questions provided in the book. The questions below are intended to get you started. These types of questions will also appear in later chapters. Consider the following:

- How does/did your church experience make you feel?
- Are/were they good feelings or bad?
- Does/did you feel accepted or rejected by your peers?

- Do/did you feel fulfilled as a person?
- Do/did you feel secure or restless?

These emotions you experienced may still be with you, even if you are not experiencing them in the present moment. We will go over this in detail. We will also go over the Christian phenomenon in order to help those who are perplexed as to the reason why they became involved with a church in the first place and why certain things did or did not happen.

Here are some more items to consider:

- When you have an emotional reaction from an interaction with another person, how do you process those feelings?
- Do you mentally categorize your feelings about people and store that in your memory for future reference?
- Do you hold the feelings in your heart and stomach and become emotionally involved?

There isn't any right or wrong answer to these questions. Just try to feel the emotions that you have experienced and how they have affected and continue to affect your life experiences. We are a composite of our life experiences and the emotions associated with them. Throughout this book, we will learn how to rid ourselves of unwanted emotions from the past. My wish for you is that you come to experience new joy and peace in order to help yourself and others live more meaningful lives and reach the highest potential.

PART 1

Subtle Energy, the Chakra System, Life after Death, Spirit, Souls

CHAPTER 1

SUBTLE ENERGY AND HOW IT WORKS

Everything begins with and is made from subtle energy. Think of the last time you drank a hot cup of coffee or tea. Do you remember the rolling steam, the warmth on your palms, and the aroma rousing your senses? Do you remember the sound as you set your cup down and savored that first sip? Our senses are stimulated by subtle energy. Hold out your hand and blow on it. The tickle and sensation on your skin is another example of subtle energy. Walk outside on a sunny day and notice the warmth from the sun on your face. This is subtle energy. Other examples of applied subtle energy are the various forms of martial arts that use chi as a means of empowering oneself. Everything we see and experience is tied to subtle energy. It is the fundamental source of energy for our spiritual experience, existence, and the universe. Subtle energy provides the building blocks for all other energy.

As previously mentioned, I was involved with Christian churches for twenty-five years and never received a satisfactory explanation as to who God is and the purpose of God's existence. I believe the answers to questions involving spirituality can be answered through understanding how subtle energy works. I am not a scientist; I have extrasensory perception, which gives me the ability to see energy fields, hear energy tones, and feel energy vibrations beyond what are considered the normal five senses. I was born with this ability but ignored it as a child because I didn't understand it or know anyone who could explain it. I was considered "too sensitive." Now, I am steadily learning more and more and using it not only for healing purposes but to also explain what I perceive to be the workings of subtle energy and how it relates to spirituality.

A basic understanding of subtle energy enables us to understand how this energy, the universe, and the concept of divine consciousness operate in our lives. It's important to eliminate the mystical perceptions of spirituality and break it down into what it really is: energy manifested in many ways, shapes, and forms. These shapes and forms are categorized and labeled differently by each culture according to its understanding and perception.

What Is God?

How did God's existence begin? It began with a single point of subatomic subtle energy forming a consciousness of its own; to give it a title, we will use "Prime Creator." This title was selected because it's a neutral term without religious connotation. When I use the word *consciousness*, I am referring to a field of energy and its ability to retain memory and to perpetuate and sustain itself. For example, a field of energy could be compared to a computer chip, as it is programmed to retain specific information.

I do not know specifically where within the universe the Prime Creator originated or when it started, but this divine consciousness inhabits the billions of galaxies of the universe. *Divine consciousness is the universal field of subtle energy that accumulates and holds information and can be used to oversee and aid the universe, earth, and our lives.* (This is referred to by some as the infinite mind.)

The Purpose for Existence

The purpose for existence is to experience all things possible. The Prime Creator is an energy field of consciousness that has the ability to manifest energy forms of various shapes and sizes. Humans, plants, animals, crystals, and minerals each have their own field of consciousness that holds their form together. This is accomplished through molecular structure. These energy forms may be organic or inorganic in nature, but they all contain their own energy fields of consciousness.

The energy forms that manifest into living beings learn to adapt to their environment. Scientists continue to discover new oceanic life forms they once believed couldn't exist. *The Prime Creator is the source of a field of subatomic subtle energy or the creative substance that has infinite power.* It has no boundaries and consists of positive and negative polarity. Our universe is comprised of subtle energy, forming patterns that manifest into vibration frequencies, such as light expressed in the various colors of the rainbow, sound vibrations, earth's magnetic fields, and gravity in our solar system.

We are spiritual beings of energy originating from the Prime Creator. Our spirits and souls are an extension of the Prime Creator and are here to experience all things possible. Energy constantly moves because the universe is in a constant state of evolution. The Prime Creator is experiencing more and more as we experience more and more, because we are a small part of the whole. This is what is referred to as the law of divine oneness. This is explained in detail in the following chapter.

Our Connection to the Universe

To understand how our energy fields of consciousness interact with the universe, we need a basic understanding of energy patterns. Subtle energy works in vibration frequencies separated into what I refer to as an octave. There are twelve octaves of vibration within a dimension. For example, compare this concept to a piano. One octave includes major and minor notes, as well as sharps and flats. Each scale is considered its own octave. In this case, there are a vast number of frequencies in each dimension. The piano is limited on notes; however, imagine the universe within each note, so to speak. There are millions of frequencies connected with the universe. The universe is a vast network of energy dimensions with a countless number of octaves and frequencies operating within it.

Dimensions of Energy

There are ten dimensions contained in the energy field that surrounds the earth. The energy vibrations we experience as a human being are the octaves within the third dimension. Earth

Mind, the crystalline field of consciousness located in the earth that holds its own chakra system of consciousness often referred to as Mother Earth, or Gaia, operates in the first dimension. All dimensions above the third are sometimes referred to as the heavenly realms. Energy flows from positive to negative in a circular fashion. When enough energy converges, it creates what is referred to as a standing wave. When enough standing waves of energy converge and take a form, things such as thought patterns and material substances manifest.

For example, our atoms are created from standing waves, which results in the molecular structure of our DNA. Energy forms, referred to as the supernatural, exist outside of the third dimension. *Something that we perceive as a spirit or ghost is the manifestation of an energy form that originates from another dimension and has a different energy vibration.* Its vibration of energy can be higher or lower than our own.

The Human Body

Our bodies are composites of subtle energy. We are like living computers with silicon-dioxide molecules, salts, and water in every body cell. Approximately sixty to seventy percent of the human body is liquid. Body fluids act as a liquid-crystal storage disk that holds our information. Our consciousness (or thought patterns) is vibrating subtle energy waves in a crystalline grid on the molecular level. Everything we feel, think, and experience is stored as cellular memory. We are a magnificent creation.

Universal Consciousness and Spirit Source

The Prime Creator formed universal patterns and cycles of energy that are relatively constant throughout the universe. They hold our universe in a unified form of existence. This intelligence of the Prime Creator is referred to as universal consciousness. The universal consciousness maintains balance by established universal laws (something that is constant and doesn't change), which allows it to operate within certain parameters. *I will use the term* Spirit Source *often in this book as a collective term for the specific subtle energy connected from Prime Creator to our spirits and souls.* It provides aiding energy specifically to our souls and spirituality. It is our connection with Prime Creator. This energy can be from—but not limited to—angels, guardians, ascended masters, and other spiritual beings. Next we will discuss universal laws that help explain the dynamics of spiritual principles.

Summary

- Spirit Source is specific subtle energy connected from the Prime Creator to our spirits and souls. It is aiding energy for our souls and spirituality, as well as for our connection with Prime Creator. This energy can be from, but not limited to angels, guardians, ascended masters, and other spiritual beings.
- Consciousness is a form of memory holding an energy pattern (i.e., standing waves).
- God's/Prime Creator's existence began with a single point of subatomic subtle energy forming its own

consciousness. It is an energy field of consciousness with infinite power, no boundaries, positive and negative polarities, and the ability to manifest energy forms of various shapes and sizes (which have their own energy fields of consciousness). To avoid a religious connotation, the term *Prime Creator* will be used throughout the book to reference this concept.

- Divine consciousness is the universal field of the Prime Creator that holds all information and can be used to aid the universe, earth, and our lives.

- We are spiritual beings of energy originating from the Prime Creator.

- The purpose of existence is to experience all things possible with the Prime Creator.

- Subtle energy works in vibration frequencies, divided into octaves.

- We operate in the third dimension. Subtle energy flows from positive to negative in a circular fashion. When enough energy converges, it forms a standing wave. Standing waves can manifest as forms such as thought patterns or material substances.

- Energy forms, referred to as the supernatural, exist outside of the third dimension. Something that we perceive as a spirit or ghost is the manifestation of an energy form that originates from another dimension and has a different energy vibration.

- Our bodies are a composite of subtle energy and are like living computers.

- Universal consciousness is the intelligence of the Prime Creator, and it uses the established universal laws to maintain balance.
- The laws of the universe are constant and do not change. They are the fundamental principles that explain how energy works and interacts within the universe.

CHAPTER 2

THE UNIVERSAL LAWS

The universal laws are thought to have their beginning with the ancient Egyptian civilizations. They provide perspective on how subtle energy works to maintain order and give balance and harmony here on earth as well as in the universe. There are more universal laws than what are mentioned in this book. I am focusing on the law of love and the twelve laws outlined in the book by Dr. Norma Milanovich and Dr. Shirley McCune: *The Light Shall Set You Free*. For further information about the universal laws, this book is an excellent reference.

Below are the principles of each law with an abbreviated definition based upon my personal experience with each of them. I believe there is value in learning these laws. They allow us to understand why things are happening to us based on how energy interacts within itself, the universe, and us.

1. Law of Love
The vibration of love is the power from the Prime Creator that allows coexistence and harmony for all beings. The love that Jesus refers to in scripture is the energy from the Prime Creator that resonates with our heart chakra to the world. The concept of love that Jesus taught allows all things and life

forms to exist in harmony, which is also known as unconditional love.

2. Law of Oneness

We live in a world where everything is connected. We are connected to the Prime Creator, which is the energy of the universe that creates all things, and we are part of it. We have an active part in what is going on in the universe, especially earth. The belief that a person's actions do not affect others is false. Individual actions affect the entire world and universe.

3. The Law of Changing of Energy/Transmutation

This law begins with this principle of energy: *When energy is converted from passive to active energy, it is transmuted or changed into another form.* The energy in our lives changes continuously. Thoughts are energy; we change energy by changing our thoughts and controlling them, as well as actions, beliefs, and words. The manifestation of our energy is found in our thoughts, belief systems, speech, and actions. When we think harmful thoughts, we send harmful thoughts to others. To change this pattern, the beginning step is to clear ourselves of the energy of past harmful thoughts and feelings. *Jesus introduced this through the concept of repentance or deciding to change one's ways.* Utilize the law of attraction; as we change our ways, we influence others to change with us.

4. Law of Correspondence

Everything exists simultaneously. All planes of existence affect each other. All are one and correspond to one another. All occur simultaneously. *The frequency the Prime Creator operates on is connected with all other planes of consciousness and is not separated by time and space.* The Prime Creator energy is within you, not at some required location (such as a church building). It is available anytime and anywhere.

5. Law of Cause and Effect

This law is the expression of divine order in the universe. Nothing escapes the law. All is in divine order. There is no such thing as chance occurrence or coincidence. The things that occur and the people we meet are for a reason. *Every cause has its effect; every effect has its cause. What comes around goes around.* This is also referred to as karma. What you do in your life whether beneficial or harmful will return to you either in this life or another to come. Understanding and respecting this law helps us during the decision-making process.

6. Law of Compensation

This is a law that helps us understand abundance and poverty and how we can approach financial matters. The law deals with material and spiritual gains or losses we receive in life. It is about giving and receiving. *For everything given, there will be a return. "It is better to give than receive."* This is where the promise of a tenfold return is found. This is the most widely misunderstood law because it doesn't pertain strictly to money. It pertains to every aspect of our lives.

7. Law of Attraction

This law extends the law of vibration because we create or attract the objects, events, and people that come into our lives. Our thoughts, feelings, words, and actions produce energies, and these energies attract like energies. Positive energy attracts positive and negative attracts negative. The law demonstrates the power of the mind, heart, and will to project what is within us, and the universe responds to this energy. This is why Jesus talked so much about loving one another, even your enemies. The more love you give out, the more you receive.

8. Law of Action

We create through our thoughts, beliefs, and actions. As you believe, so shall it be. Whatever you create, you will experience. Sometimes changes are necessary to bring your desire into reality. In order to change, action is required. Set goals and commitments to reach your desired outcome.

9. Law of Relativity

We are provided with tests or problems in life. These tests are designed to assess where we are spiritually and what experiences we need to learn. The law assures that each soul will receive a series of tests designed for the purpose of strengthening his or her spiritual being. The key to this is to learn to focus and understand the purpose of your present situation and consider the past as lessons learned. The ultimate goal is to choose what is good and beneficial for advancement of the soul. Therefore, life is different for everyone. Each person has his or her own destiny to fulfill.

10. Law of Polarity

Everything is dual. There are two poles or opposites of everything found on the physical, mental, and spiritual planes. When polarity shifts, it is the expression from one extreme to the other. *That is why there is good and evil.* When we choose to change our attitudes or behavior from the continuum of extremes, we learn self-control. *Balance is the key to success for our soul to evolve, because when we have it, we become observers and learn to master our emotions.*

11. Law of Rhythm

The laws of vibration and polarity are expanded when we add the law of rhythm. Everything vibrates and moves and has two poles or opposites, and everything vibrates to a certain rhythm. The universe moves in a cyclical fashion, with energy flowing one way and then another. *This rhythm establishes seasons, cycles, stages, development, and patterns.* The cycle or rhythm applies to all aspects of the physical, mental, and spiritual planes. For every high there is a low. As above, so below.

12. Law of Gender

Masculine and feminine energies are found on all planes of the physical, mental, and spiritual. This is an expression of the yin and yang. Some call these the positive and negative aspects of life, while others refer to this relationship as polarization. The law of gender is the creative force of our world. Male polarity creates; feminine energy complements and holds the creation in form. To create in the physical world, we must balance the positive and negative within to a point of stability to hold the standing waves that are manifesting.

13. Law of Vibration

The universe is in motion and nothing rests; everything moves or vibrates. The differences between matter and energy are expressed in unique vibratory patterns. Our chakras are an example of how subtle energy vibrates at different frequencies.

My Christian Perspective

Coming from a Christian perspective, I believe the main purpose of Jesus coming to earth was to fulfill the old law given by Jehovah and to reintroduce some of the principles found in the laws of the universe, especially the law of love. Now that we've touched on the universal laws, let's read several scriptures spoken by Jesus:

The scroll of the prophet Isaiah was handed to him. Unrolling it, he found the place where it is written: "The Spirit of the Lord is on me, because he has anointed me to preach good news to the poor. He has sent me to proclaim freedom for the prisoners and recovery of sight for the blind, to release the oppressed, to proclaim the year of the Lord's favor." Then he rolled up the scroll, gave it back to the attendant and sat down. The eyes of everyone in the synagogue were fastened on him and he began by saying to them, "Today this scripture is fulfilled in your hearing." (Luke 4:17–21)

Do not think that I have come to abolish the Law or the Prophets. I have not come to abolish them but to fulfill them. (Matthew 5:17)

The main emphasis from the above scriptures is that Jesus came to fulfill the scriptures (the Ten Commandments in the Old Testament) by introducing the law of love. He also taught principles of the other universal laws. Universal laws explain why the law of love works. Through his teachings, he showed people that they were no longer obligated to be prisoners of religious thought. They were then free to open their minds and were set free from the Old Testament laws that had kept them in conformity to religious doctrine.

Respecting and following the principle of the law of love creates harmony. For example, Jesus taught, Do to others as you would have them do to you." (Luke 6:31) Why should we "do unto others"? The answer is because of the law of cause and effect: whatever you put out comes back to you. Using the universal laws for the betterment of all equates to universal love (i.e., law of love).

Most of the universal laws have only been partially taught worldwide due to religious ignorance or oppression. Jesus tried to teach and demonstrate these laws, but many of his teachings have been distorted, destroyed, and hidden from the masses so that organized religion can maintain control over the world.

Understanding the dynamics of energy enables you to understand why the world is the way it is! Next we discuss how energy works within our bodies.

Summary

- The law of love states that the vibration of love is the power from the Prime Creator that allows coexistence and harmony for all beings; it is also known as unconditional love.
- The law of oneness states that everything is connected. Every action affects the world.
- The law of changing of energy states that when energy is converted from passive to active energy, it is transmuted or changed into another form.
- The law of correspondence states that everything exists simultaneously. Energy and planes of consciousness exist everywhere and are not separated by time and space.
- The law of cause and effect states that everything falls under divine order. Every cause has an effect; every effect has a cause. What comes around, goes around.

- The law of compensation states that for everything given, there will be a return. This is not limited strictly to finances. It encompasses every aspect of our lives.
- The law of attraction states that like attracts like. We receive the same type of energy we create. Negative attracts negative; positive attracts positive.
- The law of action states that as we create through our desire, will, and intent, action is needed on our part.
- The law of relativity states that we are provided with tests or problems in life. These tests assess our spiritual development and help us grow and progress.
- The law of polarity states that everything is dual. There are two poles or opposites for everything. This is why there is good as well as evil.
- The law of rhythm states that everything vibrates and moves, has two poles or opposites, and has a certain rhythm. Rhythms establish seasons, cycles, stages, development, and patterns.
- The law of gender states that there are both masculine and feminine balanced energies on all planes of the physical, mental, and spiritual.
- The law of vibration states that the universe in is motion and never rests.

CHAPTER 3

CHAKRAS AND THEIR STRUCTURE

The human body consists of subtle energy fields known as chakras. An aura contains the chakras and holds all of the energy. It is like an energy bubble around the human body. Chakras expand and contract as energy is utilized, and therefore, the aura expands and contracts as well. There are twelve chakras, discussed in detail in the next chapter. Some people are sensitive enough to hold their hands around a person and feel their aura energy. Auras produce light. There are cameras that capture aura colors and illustrate the vibrations of energy in the body. An online search for Kirlian photography will reveal many interesting photos on the topic. There are also cameras available for purchase for this purpose.

Positive and Negative Polarities

Chakras regulate positive and negative energy polarities. Subtle energy consists of positive and negative polarity and comes from the Prime Creator. Positive energy is considered masculine energy. Examples of applied masculine energy appear in our thought patterns and behavior as dominating, analytical, nonemotional/logical, paternal, and achievement-oriented characteristics. Negative polarity is considered feminine energy. Examples of applied feminine energy appear in our thought patterns and behavior as nurturing, feeling, emotional, passive, expressive, and maternal characteristics.

We all need a balance between the two types of energy. Chakra energy regulates body organs, so polarity imbalances cause disharmony in the organs and can create illness. It's important to note that when we refer to the two polarities, we are discussing chakra structure from an energy standpoint rather than discussing physiological and anatomical brain structure.

Chakra Structure

Through my experience with chakra work, I have come to understand that a chakra is comprised of six revolving sections of energy that move in circular rotating energy fields. Visualize six round bubbles of energy all connected and spinning. The top, front, and right sections are positive energy fields. The bottom, back, and left sections are negative energy fields. The right half of the chakra consists of positive masculine energy, and the left half of the chakra consists of negative feminine energy. The positive and negative energy fields must be balanced. If they are not balanced, the energy will affect organs in our body adversely.

Our body draws in energy. Subtle energy patterns enter our aura (into the high self and middle self) from Spirit Source above, from Earth Mind below (into our low self), and from our surroundings (into both sides of our aura). The entire chakra rotates clockwise. When all the chakras are rotating clockwise they are in unison, which allows energy to flow, aids the body to heal and work properly, and brings harmony to the body. (See the Chakra Structure illustration at the end of this chapter.)

Chakra Vibrations

Each chakra vibrates to a certain frequency and is associated with a color and sound. This is discussed further in the following chapter. The lower and slower the frequency, the lower the associated sound. Just like a musical scale, each chakra vibrates to a sound that we identify as a musical note. Here is a breakdown of each chakra and color as well as the musical note it corresponds to.

- root   red   C
- sacral   orange   D
- solar plexus   yellow   E
- heart   green   F
- throat   blue   G
- third eye   purple   A
- crown   violet   B

Music is an easy and basic example to explain how energy frequencies affect the human souls and spirit. Chakras not only vibrate to frequencies of sound, they are also connected with our emotions. Music is used to bring pleasure to our souls and can be a wonderful method for releasing stressful emotions. Music can also be used to manipulate and influence us, such as in church. When you listen to music, pay attention to how the vibration of music impacts your emotions. When lyrics are included and connected to the rhythm, one may find that it is easy to identify with the song and create an illusionary reality. This is the beauty of music; it allows for the opportunity to shift into a different reality based upon desire.

Summary

- The human body consists of subtle energy fields known as chakras.
- There are twelve chakras.
- An aura contains the chakras and holds all of the energy. It is like an energy bubble around the human body.
- Chakras have two polarities: masculine (right) positive energy and feminine (left) negative energy.
- We need a balance between the two polarities.
- A chakra is comprised of six revolving sections of energy that move in circular rotating energy fields.
- Each chakra is connected with our emotions, is associated with a color and sound, and vibrates to a certain frequency.

CHAKRA FACING FORWARD

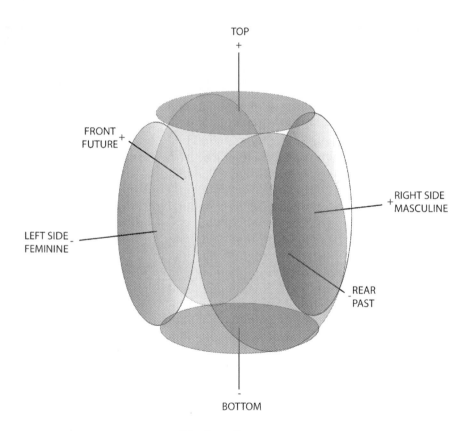

TOP
+

FRONT
FUTURE +

RIGHT SIDE
+ MASCULINE

LEFT SIDE _
FEMININE

REAR
_ PAST

_
BOTTOM

Chakra Structure

CHAPTER 4

THE CHAKRA SYSTEM

There are seven primary chakras and five secondary chakras. A primary chakra regulates energy in the body; all of the primaries together can be considered a powerhouse. A secondary chakra assists and regulates the balance of the energy in the primary chakras. Our entire chakra system is divided into three sections: high self, middle self, and low self. Each section holds its own consciousness and has its own memory field and thought forms. Illustrations are provided at the end of the chapter.

High Self

The high self is connected to our high soul (which continues on life after life) and communicates with Spirit Source. This is the spiritual part of us. The high self regulates our personality and polarities of energy. It is connected to the third eye (where we access our beliefs) and the part of us that exists after we die. It contains two secondary chakras (I AM and oversoul) as well as three primary chakras (crown, third eye, and throat). During meditation, I find that the I AM, oversoul, and crown chakras work together to bring harmony to the high self.

I AM Chakra

I AM is the highest secondary chakra. This chakra vibrates at the highest level of human consciousness and balances the manifestation of masculine and feminine polarity. As previously mentioned, energy from the Prime Creator has both positive and negative polarity, and there must be both for anything to manifest.

Oversoul Chakra

The oversoul is the center of our highest awareness. This secondary chakra works with the crown chakra to help us function as a spiritual being, and it manifests our personality, reality, and personal expression. This is where we access our assistants from Spirit Source, such as guides, angels, guardians, and ascended masters.

Crown Chakra

The crown is the seventh primary chakra, and it connects with our high self (to access higher dimensions of consciousness). It is located at the top of the head and associated with the color lavender or violet. This is where we connect with Spirit Source and receive spiritual insight. Access to this chakra is unlikely if there is a blockage in the lower chakras. The lower chakras must be cleared first. This is a safety mechanism that prevents "short-circuiting." If excessive harmful chi energy patterns from low frequencies (lower chakras) were allowed to rise into this chakra, it would create a polarity imbalance and disturb us substantially.

Third Eye Chakra

The third eye is the sixth primary chakra, and it holds the patterns or beliefs that make up our spiritual reality. It is associated with the color purple or indigo and considered to be the psychic center of the brain. It is located at the pineal gland which is connected to the hypothalamus gland. The reticular is located at the base of the brainstem and has many functions. One of them is to help balance thought patterns and body functions with the conscious and subconscious mind.

The reticular is important because during the meditation exercises later in the book, our awareness will be focused in the back of the head, where it is located. This allows our conscious thoughts to connect with the subconscious mind. We can change our beliefs by releasing old patterns of thought and introducing new ideas to our subconscious mind. Our third eye is where we learn to see with the mind's eye, perceive energy around us, and manifest patterns of thought. Our high soul is in front of our third eye. It is generally located at the front center of the head and has its own field of energy and consciousness.

Throat Chakra

The throat is the fifth primary chakra, and it is our communication center. It is associated with the color blue and located at the larynx. It involves emotions such as trust, security, creativity, expression, and receptivity. Since we eat and breathe through the throat, this is where we are nurtured physically and spiritually. The emotions produced throughout the entire chakra system are expressed here. Our verbal expression always indicates the types of emotions and energy that exist within our chakras. If we are troubled by something, the emotions and energy will manifest. For example, sometimes we can feel our throat tighten as we express difficult or stressful emotions.

Middle Self

The middle self is connected to our ego and self-identity. This is where we manifest things such as love and hate. It is considered to be the referee or the conscience between the high and low selves, and it dictates correct or incorrect choices. The middle self keeps us balanced and helps us choose between right and wrong, but it can also be involved in correct or incorrect choices. When a person is considered to have no conscience, it means that their high self is not involved in their decisions. Instead, the low self dominates by making choices without high self involvement. Therefore, our more primitive animalistic instincts dictate decisions, and the ego will support them. The middle self contains two primary chakras: the heart and solar plexus.

Heart Chakra

The heart is the fourth primary chakra, and it is connected to our emotions. It is associated with the color green and centered behind the heart organ and in front of our indwelling spirit. It is considered the zero point of energy within the body. *Heart chakra energy resonates as empathy, love, compassion, and understanding.* When a person is very loving, they radiate a strong frequency of love from their heart chakra. When you are around a person such as this, it's possible to feel this wonderful loving sensation because your heart chakra will pick up energy from theirs.

Solar Plexus Chakra

The solar plexus chakra is the third primary chakra, and it is connected to our primary expression. It is associated with the color yellow and located between the navel and heart. It is considered the "power chakra" because the ego is located here. The focus of this chakra is our primary expression toward others. If you have ever been angry and felt your abdomen tighten, then you have experienced energy produced from thought patterns that create stressful emotions in your solar plexus chakra.

Our subpersonalities develop here. A subpersonality is an adaptive personality chosen to express oneself based off of how we want to be perceived by others. Our egos and self-identities are used to create and modify our personalities to suit a particular environment. For example, a person may have three subpersonalities: one for work, one for church, one for home. That person would act differently in each setting in order to adapt to their surroundings. His or her ego and self-identity dictate the behaviors of the subpersonalities.

Low Self

The low self is connected to our instincts for survival. Everything that is passed on through biological reproduction via our DNA makeup exists here. The low self is also connected to our past life experiences on a cellular level. The energy held in the Earth Mind resonates what we experienced in our past lives. This energy carries forward into our current lives. The low self is referred to as the "animal" part of our body because our instincts rule this area. It contains two primary chakras (sacral and root) and three secondary chakras (knee, ankle, and Earth Mind).

Sacral Chakra

The sacral chakra is the second primary chakra, and it is connected with our sexual desires for reproduction and pleasure. It is associated with the color orange and located in the sacral region of our spine just below the naval. This energy supports the gonads and ovaries, and it triggers our instincts for reproduction. It is also associated with our creativity and emotional ability, including but not limited to sexual expression.

Root Chakra

The root chakra is the first primary chakra, and it is connected with our survival instincts. It is associated with the color red and located in the lower groin area. This chakra holds memory (our instincts) for survival. The emotion most associated with this chakra is fear. This is not always bad for the individual if it is related to survival. Stress related to the pressures of providing for oneself or others can be manifested in the root chakra as a knot in the stomach; this will affect the digestive system greatly.

Knee Chakra

The knee chakra is the third secondary chakra, and it is connected to plants and nature. It is located at our knees. Plants operate at a lower frequency than humans and are also sensitive to changes in energy. Plants, in addition to providing oxygen, send out soothing positive energy. Have you ever taken a walk in a forest and felt relaxed and connected with nature? Many people report feeling connected to nature while in an environment such as a forest, the mountains, a lakeside setting, by a stream, or on a beach. The reason is that your lower secondary chakras are in tune with the earth's energy fields.

Ankle Chakra

The ankle chakra is the second secondary chakra, and it is connected to rocks and minerals. It is located at our ankles. This chakra vibrates at the same frequency as rocks and minerals. Rocks and minerals have their own energy field and hold memory that is useful for transmitting energy. For example, crystals are used in meditation to direct energy. Crystals are also used in radios to transmit and receive energy waves, and in watches to generate power.

Earth Mind Chakra

The Earth Mind chakra is the first secondary chakra, and it is connected to the electromagnetic field of earth. When I meditate, I feel the top of Earth Mind resonating between the root and sacral chakras. It penetrates deep into our aura and greatly affects the low self behaviors. This chakra functions as a huge memory field, and it holds all energy from past human and animal experiences. It has a complete chakra system of its own, consisting of seven chakras total. The book of Revelation in the Bible references this as the Book of Life. It is also referred to as the akashic records of Earth Mind and Mother Earth (the feminine name Gaia).

Our conscious minds are usually not aware of these first three secondary lower chakras; however, our subconscious minds are. A person's sensitivity increases when his or her chakras are open. The more open a chakra, the more sensitive the person will be to energy.

Summary

- The aura is separated into three sections: high self, middle self, and low self.
- The aura has twelve chakras: seven primary and five secondary.
- Primary chakras regulate energy in the body.
    - crown—our spiritual connection
    - third eye—our psychic and soul center
    - throat—our communication center
    - heart—our spirit and emotion center
    - solar plexus—our primary expression connection and ego
    - sacral—our creativity and sexual center
    - root—our survival and instincts center
- Secondary chakras assist and regulate the energy within the primary chakras.
    - I AM—highest level of human consciousness; balances our polarities
    - oversoul—highest awareness center

knee—plant and nature connection

ankle—rock and mineral connection

Earth Mind—earth's electromagnetic field

connection; Earth Mind connection

- The high self is the spiritual part of us, and it oversees our personality and energy polarities. It consists of the primary chakras (crown, third eye, and throat) as well as the secondary chakras (I AM and oversoul).

- The middle self is connected to our ego and self-identity. It is the conscience or referee, and it helps us choose between right and wrong. It consists of the primary chakras heart and solar plexus.

- The low self is connected to our instincts and past life experiences. It consists of the primary chakras (sacral and root) as well as the secondary chakras (knee, ankle, and Earth Mind).

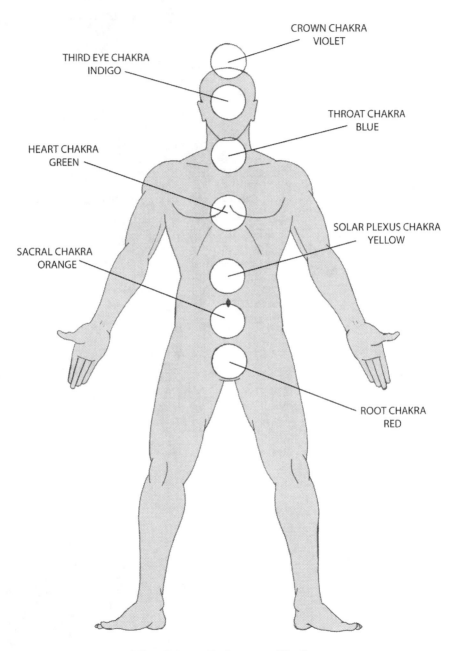

CROWN CHAKRA
VIOLET

THIRD EYE CHAKRA
INDIGO

THROAT CHAKRA
BLUE

HEART CHAKRA
GREEN

SOLAR PLEXUS CHAKRA
YELLOW

SACRAL CHAKRA
ORANGE

ROOT CHAKRA
RED

The Seven Primary Chakras

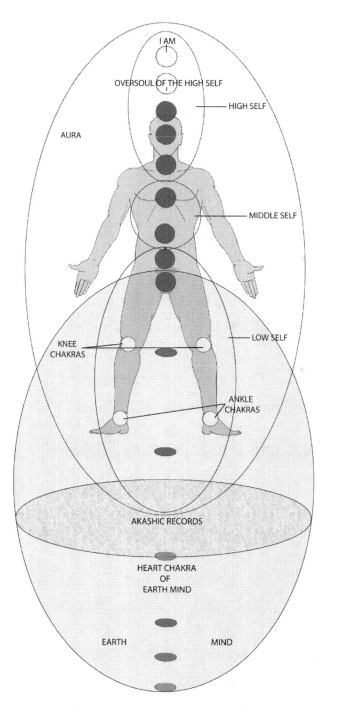

The Aura and Earth Mind

CHAPTER 5

SUBTLE ENERGY PRACTICAL APPLICATION

It is very easy and fun to check chakra rotation in the body. When our chakras are rotating together clockwise, it indicates that subtle energy is flowing harmoniously throughout the body. If we discover that some of our chakras are not rotating evenly or are rotating backward, it is an indication that our energy is out of balance. The techniques provided have been used by many people and handed down through generations of energy workers. I did not invent them.

Exercise 5.1   How to Check Chakra Rotation

To check the rotation of energy within a chakra, you will need a necklace or chain with an attached stone, crystal, or metal object (referred to in this chapter as a pendulum). Refer to the illustration at the end of the chapter. The chain needs to be flexible enough to swing easily. Lie flat on your back and dangle the pendulum above your body. It may be easier to have someone help you.

Start at the root chakra (lower groin area below your belt). The pendulum should begin to swing clockwise. This is the energy field of your root chakra. Hold it there for a minute so it has time to stabilize its rotation. Do this step for each primary chakra and note the direction of the swing for each one. Work your way up the chakras.

The sacral chakra is located at the navel. The solar plexus chakra is in the lower section of your rib cage. The heart chakra is in the middle of your chest. The throat chakra is below your chin in the throat area. The third eye is in the middle of your head, and the crown chakra is just above your head. All the chakras should rotate harmoniously clockwise, so if the necklace swings counterclockwise or does not swing at any chakra, you will want to change or begin the rotation after you are finished checking each one. We discuss how to do this in detail below.

Exercise 5.2   How to Correct Chakra Rotation

Here is a simple way to correct the energy flow of the chakras. Lie on your back and take two metal spoons or crystal points and lay one on your abdomen and the other on your chest facing up and down (parallel to) your body. Wait a few minutes and test your chakras again. The energy flowing through the spoons or crystals should redirect your chakras so they rotate clockwise.

If this method does not work after several attempts, I would suggest you visit a chiropractor and check for sublimation due to misaligned vertebrae. When vertebrae are out of alignment, it creates a disturbance in the nervous system of the body and affects the chakras. If you have never been to a chiropractor, don't be fearful. It may serve to be one of the most beneficial therapeutic experiences you will have to help achieve good health.

Exercise 5.3   How to Ground and Remove Excess Energy

Every energy field is subject to excessive amounts of energy; humans are no exception. If you feel anxious or edgy, it may be that you need to ground the energy in your body and remove excessive amounts. This exercise can be performed sitting, standing, or lying down.

In each hand hold a dark stone, or if you are fortunate to have two pieces of iron pyrite (fool's gold), that is even better. Other stones that are considered adequate for grounding include obsidian, black tourmaline, moss agate, and black onyx. If you do not have access to any of these options, then an alternative is to use two darkly colored rocks. Note that they should be dark in color because dark rocks are dense and will pull energy from your body quickly. Before using the stones, place them under running water for about thirty seconds to a minute to clear out any old accumulated energy.

You may feel a pulsing in your hands. This is subtle energy leaving your body. You should feel yourself relax as your body releases energy. Hold the stones until your hands stop pulsing. I have two pyrite stones next to my nightstand that I use often when retiring for the night. Within five minutes, I can feel my body relax as I start to drift into sleep. If I awaken in the middle of the night and thoughts flood my mind, I will hold the pyrite in my hands, and the energy will slowly decrease so I can return to sleep.

There is another technique that is widely used for grounding subtle energy from the body. I like to be standing when I do this exercise. Visualize that you have a cord or rope connected to the base of your tailbone. Imagine it is going down into the earth and connecting with the center of the earth. Now direct your energy down the cord into the center of the earth. You will begin to experience a heavy feeling as though you are connected with the ground. This is an indication that you are grounding the excessive energy from your body. When you feel relaxed, imagine disconnecting the cord from your body.

Exercise 5.4 How to Clear Energy from an Aura

This is a fast and effective exercise with several steps that you can perform on your own to clear the energy fields in your aura. Sit in a chair or use a sitting yoga position if you choose. (Refer to the illustration at the end of the chapter.)

Step 1: Take two metal spoons. Hold a spoon in each hand with the curvatures in the palms of the hands and both ends pointing to the right. As an alternative, hold two crystal points on your lap, one in each hand with the points facing to the right. This empties excessive energy from the body. Hold them until you feel your hands stop pulsing or for three to four minutes.

Use this technique to allow excessive energy to leave the aura by directing it out the positive right side of your chakras.

This clears the frontal lobes (the reasoning center of the brain). As you hold your spoons or crystals during this exercise, you will notice that your mental clarity and concentration improve. This is helpful when you desire general clarity or when you need clarity about a specific matter, especially when trying to organize daily activities.

It is not recommended, but if you reverse the spoons or crystals and face them both to the left, you will notice a flow of energy coming in from the right side, overloading the chakras with positive energy. I feel a buildup of energy that results in a headache. To correct this, turn the right spoon outward so that both spoons face outward in order to balance the positive and negative energy in your chakras.

Step 2: Take the spoons or crystals and *face them outward on each side of your lap.* This clears the left and right sides of your chakras. Hold them in that position for at least one minute.

Step 3: Hold the *left spoon or crystal backward on the left side of the waist and the right spoon or crystal pointing outward with the right hand in front of your heart.* This empties the front and back chakra fields of energy. Hold this position for at least one minute.

Step 4: *Hold with the left hand the spoon or crystal facing downward between your legs and in the right hand the other spoon or crystal upward on top of your head facing upward.* This clears the energy from the zero point of the heart chakra upward and downward. Hold this position for at least one minute.

Step 5: To fill your chakras up with new energy, *place the spoons or crystals on your lap and hold each hand facing inward.* Focus your thoughts (intent) on directing new, clean energy into your aura. This directs new energy into your chakras. There is no time limit on doing this; just hold them there until you feel you are balanced with energy.

Exercise 5.5   How to Clear a Chakra

This is a good exercise to do at the end of the day, especially if you feel stressed out. This exercise is used to clear unnecessary energy from your chakras. You can use two crystal points or two metal spoons.

Sit in a chair, or lotus position. (Refer to the illustration at the end of the chapter.)

Step 1: Start by holding a spoon or crystal in each hand and point them *straight down on each side of your legs*. If you are sitting in a chair, point them down on each side of your legs. You are now directing excessive energy from your body into the Earth Mind chakra.

Step 2: Hold a spoon or crystal in each hand and point them *outward above each side of your head*. You are now directing excessive energy outward from your crown chakra. Hold the position for about one minute.

Step 3: Hold a spoon or crystal in each hand and point them *outward on each side of your head next to your temples*. You are now directing excessive energy outward from your third eye chakra. Hold the position for about one minute.

Step 4: Hold a spoon or crystal in each hand and point them *outward on each side of the middle of your throat*. You are now directing excessive energy outward from your throat chakra. Hold the position for about one minute.

Step 5: Hold a spoon or crystal in each hand and point them *outward on each side of your chest.* You are now directing excessive energy outward from your heart chakra. Hold the position for about one minute.

Step 6: Hold a spoon or crystal in each hand and point them *outward above each side of your lower rib cage.* You are now directing excessive energy outward from your solar plexus chakra. Hold the position for about one minute.

Step 7: Hold a spoon or crystal in each hand and point them *outward above each side of your navel.* You are now directing excessive energy outward from your sacral chakra. Hold the position for about one minute.

Step 8: Hold a spoon or crystal in each hand and point them *outward above each side of your lower groin.* You are now directing excessive energy outward from your root chakra. Hold the position for about one minute.

This concludes the technique for clearing the chakras. Once you are finished, move on to the next exercise to fill your chakras with new energy.

Exercise 5.6   How to Fill a Chakra with Energy
This next technique is to fill your chakras with new energy. Use the same spoons or crystals that you used for the previous exercise to direct energy outward. In this exercise, you will follow the same eight steps; however, point the spoons or crystals

inward instead of outward. By doing so, you are directing energy inward to your chakras instead of outward. Omit step one.

Exercise 5.7   How to Program a Crystal

I am often asked, How do we know if we're filling the chakras with good or bad energy? If you are going to use the spoons, then you need to choose an environment where you are alone and feel relaxed. Find a place that is shielded from television, loud music, or a gathering of people. Coffee shops are not a good place to do this since there is a variety of energy from people and machines. Learn to be sensitive to your environment and find a place where you feel comfortable opening yourself up to receive new energy.

If you have crystals, you can program them to only allow clear energy to enter your chakras. Take each of your crystal points and run them under the facet in cold water for a minute. This will clear all excessive energy from them. Next, take the crystal and hold it in your dominant hand. Place the point in the middle of your hand and the other end against your middle finger.

Focus your attention into the crystal as if you were talking to it. Ask the crystal to empty all harmful negative energy from your chakras and only allow clear, beneficial energy to enter your body. You may find that squinting while you do this is helpful as it's important to put your entire intent into the crystal. Crystals can hold subtle energy in the form of thought patterns, and they will respond to your intent. If you use spoons, focus your intent to only allow clear energy into your aura.

Exercise 5.8   How to Shield an Aura

It is important to learn to shield your aura from harmful energy. To do so, *visualize a spiral white light rising from below your feet and rotating upward* around your feet, ankles, calves, knees, thighs, and up through each of your chakras until it flows over your head and down both sides of your body, all the way down under your feet and rotating back upward again and again. This is called "chi" or negative feminine energy from Earth Mind.

Next, *visualize a spiral white light descending from above your head and rotating down* through the crown chakra and working through all the chakras until it has passed your feet. Imagine it circling upward in front of and behind you and reconnecting with the energy above the crown chakra. This is the positive masculine energy from Spirit Source. *Visualize both energies merging and filling your body with renewed energy. Visualize a white-and-gold colored light coming down from above that covers your entire aura.* Imagine that it is a bubble of light shielding your aura from harmful energy.

When I perform this exercise, I say to my angels and guardians, "My aura is now protected from all harmful energy. Only beneficial energy can enter or leave my aura. No harmful energy is allowed to enter my aura. Thank you for the protection."

Summary

- Use a pendant to check chakra rotation. Chakras should rotate clockwise. If they rotate counterclockwise, correct the energy flow with spoons or crystals (exercises 5.1 and 5.2).

- Grounding is known as eliminating excessive energy in the body. To do so, use two darkly colored rocks or imagine a cord connecting from the tailbone to Earth Mind (exercise 5.3).
- Use spoons or crystals to clear the chakras and/or aura of excessive or harmful energy (exercises 5.4 and 5.5).
- Use spoons or crystals to recharge the chakras and aura. Program the crystals to only allow beneficial energy to enter your chakras and aura (exercises 5.6 and 5.7).
- Shield the aura by visualizing being enveloped and protected in a white light (exercise 5.8).

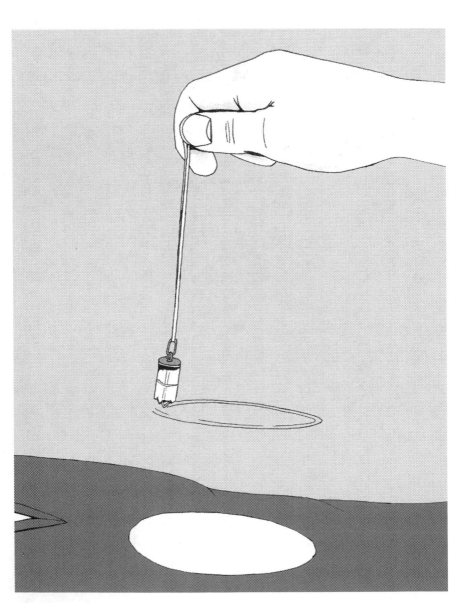

Exercise 5.1

Exercise 5.4

Exercise 5.5

CHAPTER 6

LIFE AFTER DEATH

The concept of reincarnation allows us to understand that we have more than one opportunity to live and experience life on earth. Coming from a Christian perspective, I would like to use a scripture that Jesus quoted to emphasize the fact that we are more than mere mortal humans: "Jesus answered them, 'Is it not written in your Law, I have said you are gods?'" (John 10:34).

This seems to be a widely ignored scripture spoken by Jesus, because in Christianity, there is a lack of understanding concerning the idea about our souls and eternity. Jesus is emphasizing that our souls live on continuously, therefore referring to us as gods. Our souls live on after death. They have come here to experience living on earth, and they reincarnate to experience the lessons we want to learn.

I believe that Jesus, by saying that we are gods, indicates that not only are our souls eternal but that we have the power to create as well. We did not create the universe, but our souls and spirits are a part of the Prime Creator. One of the primary functions of our existence is to be cocreators with the Prime Creator. I will explain more about this later.

When the physical body dies, the low soul (located in the low self), the energy of the middle self (which can attach/merge to either the low soul or high soul), and/or the high soul (located in the high self) can join together with the indwelling spirit, travel into a higher dimension, and communicate with Spirit Source. Therefore, our physical body may be dead, but our consciousness continues to live on.

Another scripture that is commonly used to persuade believers that man has only one opportunity to live on earth is Hebrews 9:27, which reads, "Just as man is destined to live once, and after that to face judgment." This is the scripture that holds the doctrine by Christianity that man has one chance on earth to get it right or he will either go to hell or heaven. What I believe the scripture means is that in this lifetime, in this human body, we are appointed to live in it once on earth, and then we are subject to "the judgment," which means after physical death our souls are evaluated by themselves and by their soul group as to how we performed on earth.

Christianity teaches the belief that there is an all-knowing, ever-present, almighty, and loving God who condemns the soul to everlasting hell if it doesn't get it right in its one life. What about all of the people who didn't get the chance to be a Christian? What happens to them? I've asked these questions over the years, and the usual answer was, "God is just. We shouldn't question what God considers just." I couldn't, and still cannot accept this as an adequate answer, because I believe we are here to learn and understand the meaning of life.

It has been stated by theologians that the concept of reincarnation was purposefully taken out of the scriptures around AD 325 by the bishops at the Council of Nicaea.

Why were scriptural references pertaining to reincarnation not included in the Bible? Fear is the major tool for holding humankind in religious conformity.

Lack of understanding about the afterlife can create fear. If humankind were to understand that we are here to learn certain lessons and death is not permanent, fear and manipulation tactics to keep followers in conformity and obedience would be ineffective. The religious leaders in AD 325 who were responsible for Bible scripture selection understood this. Instead, it would have been to the benefit of humankind to give people the understanding that they are part of the Creator and are cocreators with the Prime Creator.

Christianity creates dependence within people to rely upon a deity greater than themselves. They are taught to believe there is someone or something looking out for them after they die. This is true, just not in the way Christianity depicts it. We have helpers from Spirit Source that are here to help us in this life and the afterlife, such as angels, guardians, ascended masters, and deceased relatives. Our deceased relatives can comfort, protect, and assist us. Our helpers empower us and help us be cocreators. They do not have ultimate power over us. We have power to work with them and we can direct their power to aide us. We have the opportunity to use our power that is given to us by the Prime Creator. Unfortunately, Christianity does not teach the concept that humans are already part of the Prime Creator and they have power within themselves to choose what they do in their afterlife.

Many religious experiences that we encounter during reincarnations can be considered opportunities for the soul to experience something new or to finish an uncompleted task from a previous lifetime. For example, perhaps someone needs to relive the act of forgiveness. A religious experience provides a chance to perfect this lesson. The subconscious mind picks up on opportunities such as this, and the soul will cooperate until the lesson is complete or until it is time to move on. The soul will recognize the right time to move on, and the person will begin to feel uncomfortable with the present situation and have a desire for change. This may be your situation in your life now. In the next chapter, we discuss more about the soul and its purpose.

Summary

- Our souls are eternal. We are here to learn and understand the meaning of life.
- Our souls are reincarnated, and we are not limited to one chance.

CHAPTER 7

THE SPIRIT AND SOULS

Our indwelling spirit is a spark of light connected to the Spirit Source, located behind our heart. It connects us with energy for our existence and is the center of our essence of being. You are part of the Prime Creator—look just behind your heart and you will find the connection with the Prime Creator within your indwelling spirit. This subtle energy empowering our indwelling spirit comes from the Prime Creator. It is the center of our being where the collection of who we are from past lives and our higher soul experience is expressed as a human. The indwelling spirit works in conjunction with our souls (our consciousness of existence). Our souls are fields of energy that can move in and out of our bodies. Although we are generally taught that we only have one soul, we actually have two: the low soul and high soul.

The Bible mentions that when the silver cord is broken we die. This is referring to our indwelling spirit. It represents that the indwelling spirit exits the physical body upon death. When the body dies, the spirit merges with the high soul and goes to a higher dimension and continues somewhere else.

Since we are reincarnated and have had many past lives, why don't we remember them? The answer is that when our high soul returns from a much higher dimension and indwells in a human body, it is affected by the lower vibrations of the third dimension (earth's vibration of frequency) in the human body and we lose our memory. Once we learn to meditate and raise our high self up into the vibration of the fourth dimension and higher, we begin to remember our past high soul experiences. As we raise our vibration through meditation, we continue to communicate with Spirit Source and its helpers, which aid us in remembering our past experiences and why we have chosen to incarnate again on earth.

A soul group consists of approximately one thousand souls that decide to help one another from life to life. They change roles throughout lifetimes. For example, in one life, one may be the father and in another life, the mother to another soul. The variance and combinations are endless, and this allows lifetimes of different experiences and lessons. Many souls have been reincarnated somewhere between one hundred to three hundred times. When I do past life readings for people, I use a dowser to count the times of reincarnation.

The High Soul

After our body dies, our high soul travels to the fourth dimension or higher and goes through an evaluation and period of reflection and learning. The high soul is usually aided by deceased relatives and angels. When I need to connect with the high soul and spirit of a deceased person, I start in the fourth dimension and ask the guardians and angels to locate the spirit. This is where I find out whether they are available to communicate. A spirit does not have to communicate if it chooses not to. They have free will.

The Low Soul

In my meditation practices, I have not been able to define the low soul as an object located in one particular location of the low self; rather, it's the energy field tied to the root and sacral chakras. When I communicate with my low soul, I take my awareness down to my root chakra. The primary means of communication with the low soul is a very simple reasoning method as though speaking to a young child. In the course of evaluating the low soul's progress, I find I generally go by the feelings I experience instead of verbal communication (which I use with my high soul).

Earth Mind is the consciousness of energy located in the electromagnetic field within the earth. Normally at death, members of their soul group in Earth Mind assist the low soul to get it back to the group, where it also goes through an evaluation and period of reflection and learning. However, the low soul is exposed to and awakened to the harmful experiences it subjected humankind to during life. Religion refers to this as hell.

Instead of a soul going to hell, it is really going to Earth Mind, where it is evaluated by itself and its soul group. The soul group helps the soul decide where, when, or if the soul will reincarnate. If intended lessons were not learned, they will be repeated in another life. Those that have committed suicide usually will have to experience a similar life once again in order to overcome the obstacles and challenges on earth that they did not want to face.

When the low soul is disciplined through the result of many reincarnations and has experienced its lessons by cooperating with the high soul, they merge as one at the time of death. If the low and high souls have evolved to a high enough state, they need not be evaluated, and they have the option to choose to return to earth or stay in the higher astral planes. They may choose to return to earth to experience something new or work with Spirit Source to help humankind, or a combination of the two.

They may instead choose to become an ascended master, working with angels, giving advice, and offering power to help people on earth reach their souls' higher purpose. Some of these ascended masters have been referred to as saints. They are not to be worshipped (although they should be respected), but rather, they should be called upon to act as coworkers helping us. I have experienced healing energy and guidance from ascended masters, and I'm very grateful for their help.

Since we come here to experience many lifetimes, we choose lifetimes of hardship or disaster to learn lessons. In some lifetimes, we are caught in a sudden traumatic death experience, and out of fear, either the high or low soul doesn't know how to cross over into another dimension to its soul group. For example, in 2011 a tsunami hit Japan. I participated in a meditation group, and we sent love to the families in Japan. We discovered there were thousands of low souls that had not yet crossed over to meet their soul groups. Sudden death had left them unprepared to leave. We assisted thousands of souls to the other side by creating a vortex of light into Earth Mind for the souls to use in order to travel back to their soul groups. Angels and guardians assisted them along the way.

The low souls that remain in the third and fourth dimensions are usually stuck or confused. Paranormal investigators call them ghosts or spirits of the dead. The only dead thing about them is their physical body. Their consciousness is usually intact. Sometimes they choose to stay in the same location of their death in an attempt to get attention (by creating disturbances) in order to receive help crossing over or perhaps to communicate a message to a loved one.

It is my experience that when the high or low souls remain in the third and fourth dimension or if they visit, they require energy in order to manifest their presence. They can appear as orbs of light, shadows, human form, or another form. They obtain energy from wherever they can. Sometimes they use people and draw energy from their auras. I will share with you a story that I experienced while working with a family:

I was working with a man, woman, and six-year-old daughter, and they had just rented a house. They moved in less than one month previous to that time. I visited them in their home, and the woman was quick to tell me that I should avoid going into the basement. She said there were spirits down there. The man had heard the voice of a young girl talking in the early hours of the morning. He investigated, thinking it was his daughter, but she was sound asleep.

I began dowsing the house and discovered three low souls in the basement. I went into the basement and was greeted by a grandfather, a father, and a young girl about the age of eight. The house had been built in the 1920s, and the girl had died of an illness in the house sometime in the 1930s. Her low soul remained in the house. Her grandfather and father's low souls were there to comfort the girl. I crossed these souls over to their soul group and they left the house.

What I feel is especially important in this story is that the man and woman's six-year-old daughter had recently developed a medical condition that was depleting the energy in her body. The girl would wake up in the morning very tired. The medical doctors instructed her to wear an oxygen monitor at night to monitor her oxygen levels. They discovered during the early hours of the morning, her oxygen levels would severely drop and cause extreme fatigue. The low soul of the deceased young girl in the basement was using the living child's energy. After I crossed the low souls over, her condition returned to normal and she is now healthy and strong.

Take comfort in knowing that you are only separated from your deceased loved one's high soul by unseen dimensions and that you are still connected to that person through your love for him or her in your heart. It is possible to feel the person's love for you as well. It's important to remember to focus your life on what you came here to accomplish. It can be difficult to go on with life after losing a loved one, but remember: you have a purpose on earth! Time is nonexistent in other dimensions. You will have all the time you want with them, and they will be there for you when you're finished on earth.

I have the ability to communicate with spirits. I was with my father when he passed over, and I was able to help his low soul make the transition without fear. He was in a hospital, unconscious from a brain hemorrhage. His nervous system was still operating, meaning his spirit and low soul were still present. His high soul had already departed to a higher plane of consciousness. I communicated with his low soul and the spirits of deceased family members that arrived in the room to be with him. I recognized my grandfather and grandmother. Uncles and aunts were there as well. I communicated with my father's low soul regarding the lessons he had learned while on earth, and we departed with a loving "good-bye for now." The next day his high soul appeared as a ball of light energy. My mother's high soul was there with him. They told me that everything was fine, and I should continue to help others understand the afterlife.

I've had many opportunities to help souls cross over to their soul group. I visited a home that was built over a Native American burial ground dating back 150 years. Apparently the chief of the tribe presented himself as an apparition to one of the residents of the home. The residents were unsettled by the occurrence, and I volunteered to look into the matter. I communicated with the chief and offered my assistance. He allowed me to help him and members of his tribe return to their soul group and be reunited with their relatives. I created a vortex for them to use and counted thirty-nine souls, escorted by their ancestors, enter the vortex to cross over.

A Ghost Named Herman

Before I begin a session of energy work on a person, I do a preliminary reading on them. I get permission from their angels, check for entities, and gather general information from my guides that will be helpful for the person. This usually takes me fifteen to thirty minutes.

I was preparing to meet a lady when a spirit appeared before me. It was the face of a man in his sixties with a gray beard and uncombed gray hair. He sort of resembled what I would imagine to be a sea captain. I asked him who he was and he answered, "Herman is my name."

Usually once the high souls and spirits of deceased relatives of the person I'm working with discover that I have the ability to communicate with them, they will show up, hoping to communicate with their family member. But I soon discovered that Herman was not a relative of the lady coming to see me. After I spoke to him, he just faded away.

During the session with the lady, I asked her if she had a relative named Herman. She said no, but the only Herman she knew about was a ghost that she named that lived on the sailboat she had owned.

The lady and her husband had owned a yacht and were sailing around the world. Her husband became very ill and was in the hospital in Singapore and she was living on the yacht. She and her husband decided to sell the yacht. Every time she would go to the forward compartments, she noticed a foul smell. She checked everywhere but couldn't find any reason for the smell. She finally recognized that this was the doing of a spirit, whom she named Herman.

She came to an agreement with Herman that he would leave her alone if she would live in the aft of the yacht and he could have the front. This went on for several months. Most of the time when a potential buyer came aboard, the yacht would reek with a foul odor to discourage the buyer; once the electrical system even shorted out. She finally did sell it and came back to the United States. She had been back several months when she called me for a session. As I communicated with Herman, I found out that he was the original owner of the yacht and had died on it. His high soul did not know where to go, so he followed the lady to me. Herman left cheerfully as I sent him to his angels in the higher realms.

I have learned how to use my abilities to connect with the past lives of people. I do this to help clear destructive patterns of behavior from their past lives in order to clear their karma. Karma is a result of the law of cause and effect. Everything we do on earth in a negative or positive way affects our future lives. What we did in previous lifetimes affects our present lifetime. If we made choices that created a harmful pattern in our life or someone else's, then the energy of those experiences will continue forward in time until it is changed.

When I discover a situation in a person's past life experience that is creating a disturbance in their present life, I will go back in time to the situation and change it to something beneficial. The only time I do not do this is if I have not received permission from the person's angels to change their karma. I do not want to disrupt a person's karma since they have their own life lessons to learn for themselves.

The standing waves of energy that hold that past life situation can be changed as I go back in time and relive the situation and replace the energy field with a beneficial situation.

I call it the right choice instead of the wrong choice. I change the situation so the karma produces unconditional love, and I carry it forward in time to the present. When I do this, it clears their karma and allows them to live free of the past life that was creating a problem for them. When I identify this problem and inform the person about their past life experience, it helps them understand the lesson that needed to be corrected, then they can be careful not to repeat the same behavior in this lifetime.

To give you an example, I was working with a lady who experienced extreme anger toward a family member. It involved a certain offense related to one of her children's marriage. This anger would repeatedly surface and would affect her sleeping pattern. I found the past life experience from several hundred years ago that was troubling her.

She had been a single woman in her twenties and was engaged to a man. She was living with her mother at the time, and her mother didn't want her to get married. The mother deliberately created a problem with the fiancé and discouraged him from marrying her daughter. The fiancé broke the engagement and found someone else to marry. The daughter was angry with the mother and never forgave her for what she did. The energy produced from this anger carried forward into the lady's present lifetime. The anger contained in the past life experience was triggered in the lady by the present life event.

I went back to the time when the daughter and the man first started dating. I changed the situation so that the mother did not interfere with the engagement, and they were happily married. I brought forward unconditional love to the present time, and her anger disappeared and has not returned.

Morbid Ghost Stories

Some people experience tragic deaths and need assistance crossing over to their soul group. I was asked to visit a boutique shop that had peculiar activity. A vender rented a wall in the store to display antique china, and her antique china cups were supernaturally thrown across the room and broken. Needless to say, she left the business. When the owners of the business vacuumed the floor, they could hear a woman screaming. Fortunately the owners were sensitive enough to investigate what was going on in the building.

As I drove up into the strip mall, I was shown the story of the situation at hand by my angelic helpers. About seventy-five years before that time and before the strip mall had been built, there was a farmhouse on the property, where a husband and wife lived. One night a man entered their house and hit the husband on the head, subdued him, and tied him up. He brutally beat the woman and then killed the husband in front of her so she had to witness her husband's death. Then he molested the woman and killed her.

As I was shown these past events, I felt the suffering and pain inflicted upon these people as they were murdered. The sudden trauma had prevented them from crossing over to their soul group. They had been stuck in this time period for many years, reliving this situation and trying to find someone to help them cross over.

Once I entered the store, I immediately connected with the high souls of this couple. I heard the wife say to her husband, "Finally there is someone here to help us." The high souls had created disturbances in the store to get the attention of the store owners. Tears ran down my face because of the pain of their experience, even as I explained the process of crossing over. They thanked me and were grateful as their angels assisted them into a vortex allowing them to go to their soul group.

Another experience occurred in a private residence that was in a subdivision built on what once was a crematorium in the early 1900s. There was a high amount of spiritual activity in this house, and in the course of three hours, I crossed twenty-seven low souls over. The one that was most startling to me was the low soul of a boy about the age of eleven years old. He came forward from a group of children who were huddled in the corner of a room. I asked him why he was alone. He told me he had run away from home because he didn't get along with his parents. He met a farmer and agreed to work for him for room and board. As he was telling me his story, in my mind I went back in time with him and was shown what had happened to him.

The farmer was a cruel man in his forties who took the boy into his barn and beat and molested him. The boy told the man that if he didn't stop the abuse, he would go to the authorities. The man took a knife and killed the boy. I was experiencing this situation as an observer from a short distance and feeling the pain and suffering of the child. The man looked in my direction and started cursing. I was so angry that I asked the angels permission to send him to the lower realms of Earth Mind.

I was told to let him be and not disrupt his karma. I was there to help the child cross over to be with his soul group. I helped the boy to be reunited with his family and soul group. This kind of energy work is not a glamorous or pleasant task. Afterward, it leaves me numb until I completely empty myself from the disturbing energy.

Summary

- The indwelling spirit is a spark of light within us that is connected to the Prime Creator. It works in conjunction with our souls and connects us with energy for existence.
- It's possible to regain our memories from past lives once we reconnect with the Prime Creator and Earth Mind.
- A soul group is a group of souls that have decided to help one another from life to life.
- Earth Mind is the consciousness of energy located in the electromagnetic field within the earth.
- When we die, the low soul goes to Earth Mind if it didn't complete all necessary lessons intended while on earth. It evaluates the time spent on earth as does its soul group. Any incomplete lessons will be repeated in the next life on earth.
- When we die, the indwelling spirit joins the high soul and travels to other dimensions. There they evaluate, reflect, and learn from the time spent on earth.

- If the low soul completed all lessons while on earth, it joins and merges with the indwelling spirit, middle self, and high soul and has the freedom to move to higher dimensions or return to earth to work with Spirit Source to help others as a spiritual guide or ascended master.

- Karma is result of the law of cause and effect.

PART 2

Earth Mind, Collective Consciousness, Spirit, Soul, Life after Death, Works of the Spirit

CHAPTER 8

EARTH MIND, COLLECTIVE CONSCIOUSNESS, THE COLLECTIVE CONSCIOUSNESS OF RELIGION

Earth Mind

The phrase, "as above so below," provided in the definition of the law of rhythm, also applies to Earth Mind. As it is in Earth Mind, so it is in our lower souls. Earth Mind is comprised of silicon dioxide and acts as a huge computer chip that holds the memory of all things on earth. A vast grid pattern of frequencies hold the information. It has recorded all energy patterns from organic matter since its beginning, and it is referred to as the akashic records.

The many lives we have spent on earth are recorded in Earth Mind, and the energy patterns of the past still resonate with our low souls and influence the low self, whether we are conscious of it or not. Many of the hereditary characteristics of your family are a carryover from the energy established in Earth Mind. Many repeated patterns of behavior by a group of people establish what I refer to as collective consciousness, which is the accumulation of the dominate energy patterns from a certain group of people, this forming (but not limited to) cultural and national personality traits. I will discuss later in the chapter how this affects our religious as well as other beliefs.

The energy patterns in Earth Mind have a profound influence upon who we are today. Each lifetime we have spent serves as an experience to teach us lessons regarding our current lifetimes. Each person is on a different level of evolutionary development and has to experience life for himself or herself.

Our low souls are directly influenced by Earth Mind continuously. Every building, city, county, state, and country has its own energy field tied to Earth Mind. Have you ever noticed how you feel different when you go to various places? You are constantly influenced by Earth Mind energy from people, animals, plants and trees, rocks and minerals, oceans, lakes, and rivers. A certain place may feel peaceful or disturbing, or perhaps it may trigger a memory of a past life or a feeling that you have been at this location before, commonly referred to as déjà vu. This is simply your low self sensing energy from Earth Mind. By learning to become sensitive to your surroundings, you can discover feelings and emotions that can alert you to something that is related to your karma.

Karma is the accumulation of energy created by our actions that returns to us. It can be from a beneficial or unbeneficial action. If we have done something that created a harmful situation or outcome, that energy returns to us and we have the opportunity to recognize it as a lesson and change our actions. Beneficial situations and outcomes return in a beneficial way as positive reinforcement. It will depend upon the lessons your soul has experienced. Sometimes a place will remind you of a pleasant previous lifetime or a place where you experienced a difficult hardship. The key is to recognize the lesson and learn from it, then move on and let the past go. We have many lifetimes to come if we choose, so let's learn and look forward to what's new for us in the future.

People often move to a new location to start over with their lives. This can be beneficial, but you must release the old energy from Earth Mind from the place you left so you will be ready for new experiences. That is one of the primary purposes of this book. We will discuss clearing Earth Mind later (see chapter 22). The old energy that I am discussing is the harmful energy that creates patterns or habits in the low self, prohibiting you from achieving beneficial growth for your soul. In addition to Earth Mind energy, it's important to be aware of collective consciousness and how it affects our beliefs and energy.

Collective Consciousness

When a group of people gather and agree on an idea or concept, their energy manifests itself into what is referred to as consciousness (ability an energy pattern has to hold a form of memory within itself). When the energy of this consciousness is collected in a group setting, it is called group consciousness, or collective consciousness. Our whole world is comprised of collective consciousness in various ways. It is defined by geographical regions of the country, educational systems, advertising media, recreational sports, business corporations, and much more.

Music is an example because every style of music stimulates the emotions of a culture or subculture of people. It creates its own collective consciousness. Consider how the music you listen to affects you and your emotions. Do your religious beliefs influence the type of music you listen to or the emotional responses you have to the music? In this book, I will emphasize how collective consciousness influences humankind in the area of religion.

Most people are usually curious about new ideas and concepts unless they have been strongly influenced by a collective energy field of consciousness that teaches a specific idea as the ultimate truth. The group consciousness continues to reinforce the belief system. Truth is all relative at the particular time and space of an individual's experience. A concept or thought can be manifested into a field of energy that creates its own form of reality (for the people believing the information). To the group of people who belong to the collective consciousness, the idea that is taught is ultimate truth. It will remain true so long as they choose to believe it.

Collective Consciousness and Religion

Why do people feel they need to go to church? Some people want a sense of belonging to something bigger than themselves, which they hope will bring more significance to their lives. Remember the law of attraction: like attracts like. When people find themselves void of companionship with like-minded people, they will seek to find it.

Church is an easy place to begin because it projects the image that we all need God and we need to belong to a body of believers with common ideals. The message of hope that the churches generate creates the illusion that church is where people meet God and that it is the best place to receive the support that they are looking for. Oftentimes family members and peers influence the decision as well because they have been attending a church for years. Most people stay religious their entire lives until they experience something extremely undesirable associated with church. Your soul will continue the religious experience until it is satisfied that it has had enough. That is why some people do not have a desire to change.

There is one key factor in all of this: religious indoctrination. When people embrace the religious collective consciousness of a church, they give their personal will or power to that church. They may not consciously be aware that the teachings are manipulating them, and they are subject to the power of the collective consciousness. As they continue to be manipulated and controlled by the collective consciousness, they become less and less likely to change, unless their souls recognize that it's time to move on.

Here is an example of how the conflict between staying or leaving church can begin. Sometimes when a person is greatly offended by church members or the leadership of the church for some reason, it triggers the high and middle selves to rethink what the person is doing there. The low self responds in anger because of the offense. Here begins the struggle when the low self says, "Forget this place; I am going to find somewhere else to go." Or, "I am fed up with the whole religious experience."

If you were this person, the amount or weight of the influence the collective consciousness has on you personally determines how you would proceed. Perhaps you are not so heavily influenced and you decide to leave and find a new spiritual journey. Perhaps you leave and find another church and where you experience the same or a similar situation. Or perhaps the collective consciousness is so heavy that you give in to guilt and fear regarding failure to meet church standards, ask for forgiveness from them, choose to believe it is where you belong in order to fulfill "God's will," and stay.

If you choose to stay, you are further reinforcing the collective consciousness. Sometimes our souls need to go through this sequence several times in order to fully understand the religious experience. Remember that your soul is free to choose for itself what it wants to do. If this has happened to you, I am not criticizing you for staying; rather, I am explaining to you why and what you are doing. When the soul decides it is time to move on from your current religious experience, then the high self, with the aid of the angels or guardians assigned to you, will prompt you to look elsewhere. The difficult part is removing the instilled beliefs from the collective consciousness (tied to the emotions) so you can learn something else more beneficial for your soul. In the last section of this book, I will explain techniques that may help you rid yourself of old or harmful beliefs and emotions.

Summary

- Understanding how your low self has been influenced by your past lives can be beneficial to help you change harmful patterns.
- Earth Mind, known as akashic records, holds all information/energy patterns from all organic material, including our past lives.
- We can access our past lives in Earth Mind to help us understand our current lives.
- We are constantly influenced by Earth Mind energy.
- Every location has its own energy field tied to Earth Mind.
- Collective consciousness is the accumulation of the dominate energy patterns from a certain group of people, this forming (but not limited to) cultural and national personality traits.
- The low soul is directly influenced by Earth Mind continuously.
- By learning to become sensitive to your surroundings, you can discover feelings and emotions that can alert you to something that is related to your karma. The key is to recognize the lesson and learn from it, then move on and let the past go.
- Group or collective consciousness is manifested energy created when a group gathers or agrees upon an idea.
- The soul knows and will prompt you when it's time to change your current situation.
- Removing instilled beliefs from your mind enables you to learn and adopt new beliefs.

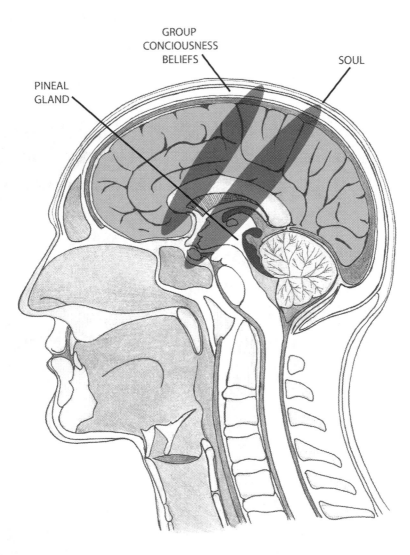

PINEAL
GLAND

GROUP
CONCIOUSNESS
BELIEFS

SOUL

Collective Consciousness and the High Soul

CHAPTER 9

MY PERSONAL EXPERIENCE

For years I would pray, "God just show me your will and I will do it." I was in India on a short missionary trip, and our group went to a village of what is referred to as the "no cast" people—those who are considered to be below the lowest cast in India. They live on the outskirts of the city in makeshift shelters. These are some of the most humble and nicest people I have ever met. Everyone was stricken by illness, so we laid hands on them and prayed, and they were all healed within hours.

Their religion was Hinduism and they had very little, if any understanding of Christianity. I was struck by the fact that Jesus would heal people who had nothing to give in return, and these people would merely add Jesus as another god to their religious portfolio instead of embracing him as the only Lord and Savior. (It would be difficult for them to renounce Hinduism and replace it with Christianity due to possible persecution by the other religious groups.)

During this time, I was praying and asking God if I was doing his will. An inner voice spoke to me and said, *You are in my will.* I now understand that was one of my angels communicating with me. I finally understood that the purpose of the trip was to experience healing as a demonstration of the unconditional love of the Prime Creator toward humankind. It had nothing to do with church, doctrines, or belief systems.

This started the process of questioning the Christian religious system, as well as serving and following what the church teaches. A possible rebuttal to this is the idea that since I was following all the doctrines of the Bible, I was able to heal the people. No, it had nothing to do with doctrine. It was my desire, intent, will, and working with Spirit Source that healed others. It manifested healing energy and healed people even though I didn't understand the dynamics of subtle energy at the time. Spirit Source will aid people when they try to help others when their desire, will, and intent are motivated by unconditional love.

I have observed that in many churches it seemed as though people were always praying for healing but usually nothing of significance ever happened. One might suggest that we didn't have faith and that is why. However, the church spent hours praying in faith for people but with few to no results. The true reason is they were not connected to the power of Spirit Source, but rather, they were blocked by the collective consciousness (full of their beliefs and concepts of healing). In 2 Timothy 3:5, Paul writes about the church in the latter days, "having a form of godliness but denying its power." The power they had was their group consciousness rather than Spirit Source.

In church it was taught that we are to be servants of God. I want to be careful here and not criticize sincere religious people for doing their best to help others and show love. Some of us came here to learn how to help humankind and to love unconditionally. I understand what it's like to have the desire to serve, and the church provides a beneficial outlet for this desire. However, connection with Spirit Source does not obligate you to anything! I understand the concept of being a servant for the Lord. *We are spiritual beings with free will—we have the freedom to make our own choices.*

Churches often want followers to believe that our purpose for being here is to serve the church. (This is another example of how collective consciousness works.) They may say if you serve the church, then you are serving God. This is not necessarily true. I have found that a church's purpose is usually centered on the leadership. You need to evaluate for yourself whether a church is operating from a place of unconditional love or some other motive. Isn't it only reasonable to evaluate the performance of a church based upon how it expresses itself in unconditional love? A church's purpose should be to help people reconnect with the Prime Creator and, through unconditional love, to be of service to humankind.

I believe if you want to be of service to humankind, you need to be reconnected to the Prime Creator and learn to become a cocreator of love with it. By doing so, you will learn to raise the vibration of humankind through love and help yourself, earth, and the universe. Also, if you can learn to clear the emotional energy of fear and obligation to serve from the collective consciousness of your church, you will allow your soul to be in a position to direct you as to what you should do next in life. Remember, it's your souls' choice.

Summary

- It's possible to use subtle energy for healing purposes regardless of your religious beliefs.
- We are spiritual beings with free will—we have the freedom to make our own choices.

CHAPTER 10

THE BORN-AGAIN EXPERIENCE

Whether religion is right or wrong for your soul is subjective. It may be necessary for your soul to go through a religious experience. I am not criticizing anyone for choosing to be religious either in the past or present. It may be the only option available for you to complete a karmic lesson. Even if religious teachings are inaccurate, your soul can still learn from the experience. When you have learned all the necessary lessons through your religious experience, your soul will become restless.

I spent twenty-five years in Christian churches and experienced many a phenomenon through the charismatic movement (more on this later). I understand what it's like to believe material taught as truth in the church and that many will continue to defend and believe it as absolute truth until their dying day. I used to be the same way, and I completely understand the mind-set. I have benefited greatly from my religious experiences. However, I have come to recognize what I believe are incorrect teachings concerning spirituality. This is based upon my greater understanding of how energy works, our connection with Spirit Source (such as working with angels), and how subtle energy is used to manipulate and control people.

Many people are familiar with modern Christianity and how it works. Here's a breakdown for those who are not: Unless people are born into it, the Christian religious experience begins for them when they are preached to and told they need a Savior because they are sinners and need to be saved. The recipients are asked to accept Jesus into their hearts, receive Jesus as their Lord and Savior, or ask God into their lives as their Savior.

What is really happening? If someone preaches to another person, their energy, as well as the collective consciousness they belong to, will challenge the subconscious mind of the recipient. Peer pressure is a possible result of collective consciousness. The presentation generally triggers guilt and/or the desire to conform, especially if the recipient of this presentation has a desire to discover and reconnect to the Prime Creator on a subconscious level.

Sometimes there are past life experiences that require further lessons, and our low self recognizes the opportunity. The challenge to make things right from a past life experience presents itself so the low self agrees with the high self to try the experience. The high self recognizes this as a potential opportunity to reconnect with the Prime Creator. The exercise of asking Jesus into the heart is not to be discredited, as a genuine reconnection may actually occur. The desire to reconnect with the Prime Creator must be expressed through the intent of the heart.

When we ask Jesus into our hearts (intent), it may feel that we are "born again" and have made progress. There very well could have been a physical experience associated with the exercise and a noticeable change from within. This is where our spirit center connects with the Prime Creator. But after this experience, this is where the confusion can begin, because if this is done through the assistance of a religion or church, it opens the door for a connection with the collective consciousness associated with that religious institution. As you begin to believe the doctrines and teachings of the church, you give your power over to the collective consciousness. The standards and beliefs of the collective consciousness dictate what you can and cannot believe—which is dangerous because you lose your personal power to the group.

There are many different beliefs about who Jesus was and is, and what is necessary to believe in order to be saved. Religious experiences are based on the group field of consciousness of the church you gave your power to. Yes, you may have had a genuine reconnection with the Prime Creator, but you will be blocked from learning directly from it because of the church's established doctrines in its field of consciousness.

Can a soul discover for itself its reconnection with the Prime Creator without religious involvement? The answer is yes! *You don't need religion or a church. You only need the reconnection with the Prime Creator to help you understand why your soul is here on earth.*

The high self desires to reconnect with the Prime Creator. For many, religious involvement begins with a desire to know more about God (the Prime Creator or what is referred to as a "higher power"). This desire to know more is our high self wishing to connect consciously to the Prime Creator because *this is where your spirit and soul came from.* The desire in your heart to connect with the Prime Creator is natural. Your spirit and soul want to be reconnected. Problems arise, however, because there are so many religious fields of consciousness developed by religious teachings, which makes it difficult to know how exactly to reconnect with the Prime Creator.

I believe it's quite simple to reconnect with the Prime Creator. Here is a simple technique to do so: Quiet yourself and bring your awareness to your heart. Be sincere and put your intent into the desire to know in your heart that you can reconnect with the Prime Creator. Focus your intent upon your desire. Say from your heart, *"I call upon the Prime Creator to reconnect with my spirit. Thank you and so it is."*

I believe *there are many ways to reconnect with the Prime Creator.* It is not limited to only one correct way. It is your intent and heartfelt desire to reconnect that matters. All that is needed is a desire for spiritual reconnection—no religious ritual required. *Reconnection is simply a conscious effort of your high self directing your spirit center to reconnect to its original source.*

To dissect the process of being "born again" or being "saved," we discover that it starts with a desire. Our soul's desire is to be reconnected with the Prime Creator. The high self, the section of the chakra system that is capable of connecting with the Prime Creator, does so during this process. In Christianity the term for "born again" is called conversion.

During the conversion process, a person will confess their sins with the intent to change their "evil" ways. What does this really mean? When your high self realizes it is connected with the Prime Creator, it attempts to raise its vibration of energy in order to become more efficiently connected. In order for this to occur, old thought patterns must be cleared. The low and middle selves will cooperate during this process and drastic changes may occur as energy rebalances within the chakras. A person will then willingly give up bad habits and change their ways according to the church standards and what is deemed to be "God's will." Remember, this is all tied to the collective consciousness of the church. The desire to change causes old or harmful energy patterns to clear out and be replaced by new beneficial energy patterns. This is the low self and middle self cooperating with the high self. This is why some people have drastic conversions when they experience the born-again phenomenon.

When energy is cleared from a chakra, it must be replaced. The law of changing of energy/transmutation is involved when the chakras are cleared of old or harmful patterns of thought and replaced with new beneficial thought patterns. However, when a person is converted—or born again—and adopts the beliefs taught by the church, some of their old thought patterns can be replaced by the energy patterns that exist in the church's collective field of consciousness.

When converts agree to follow the doctrines or tenants of the church, they give their power over. Then they are baptized and hand over even more power. Then they agree to obey a pastor, priest, rabbi, guru, or any other leader of a church and fall under their control. In most cases, people are trained to believe they must answer to these leaders for their actions, rather than discovering for themselves what is necessary for spiritual growth. It can be frustrating when a person needs real answers and only receives a limited understanding based solely on specific religious beliefs. Once you realize that your religious experience does not meet your needs any longer, it is important to learn how to release your limited beliefs and be open to new ideas that are more beneficial for your soul's development.

Summary

- The soul can reconnect with the Prime Creator without religious involvement or assistance.
- It is possible to be reconnected with the Prime Creator by being "born again"; however, the religious doctrine you accept during the process may block you from learning directly from the Prime Creator.
- The high self and soul desire to reconnect with the Prime Creator because it's where they came from.

CHAPTER 11

THE PHENOMENON OF THE WORKS OF THE SPIRIT

The topics in this chapter are introduced in accordance with what I was exposed to and practiced from a Christian-based standpoint. However, many of these topics included in the "works of the Spirit," such as the anointing, speaking in tongues, prophecies, laying on of hands, discernment of spirits, healing, and miracles, are dissected and explained with what I have come to understand based on a subtle energy work standpoint.

Anointed or Kundalini?

I usually have the ability to sense energy fields of consciousness, and when I enter a religious place of worship, such as church, I feel the collective consciousness. When a church service begins with music, my chakras are immediately stimulated and I feel energy vibrations rise. When I regularly attended church, I would experience a tingling sensation of energy that flowed down the spine. It was similar to experiencing the chills, and it gave me an energetic, euphoric feeling and opened my senses to the group consciousness within the church. I experienced this sensation almost every week at church for at least twenty-five years. I used to refer to it as a spiritual fix. No worship service was considered complete without this sensation because I was led to believe that I was really connecting with the Holy Spirit.

This was interpreted as "the anointing" coming through the Holy Spirit; however, what I've come to understand is that it's generally nothing more than the energy of people around me resonating in my chakras and stirring up emotions, which gives the impression of the Holy Spirit. The anointing experience compelled me to prophesy from time to time.

I am not attempting to discredit this type of experience, as it is very real. When we worship, we open our chakras and receive energy from our surroundings. What we feel is very real. It's important to evaluate what we feel and how it influences us in order to decide if it serves a purpose to help us reach a higher potential or if it's simply a pleasing, emotional experience. The anointing experience stimulates the chakras but does not flow completely through the body. This is where kundalini and the anointing differ, although energy pulsations and sensations may feel similar.

The kundalini experience is the connection of energy (positive) from Spirit Source that descends through our chakras, splits around our feet, and ascends back in the front and back of our aura. This repeats many times. Negative energy, from Earth Mind (chi), ascends through our chakras, splits above our head, and descends back down the perimeter of our aura. This flow repeats many times as well. This process clears old and harmful patterns of energy from the chakras and energizes the body. Refer to the illustration at the end of the chapter.

I have experienced both the anointing and kundalini flows while in worship services. Spirit Source used the religious setting to help clear my chakras so that I would be prepared to be open to question my religious experiences. Kundalini helps clear the chakras to bring mental clarity, whereas the anointing is simply a stimulation of chakras that reinforces group consciousness. I continue to experience kundalini flows during meditation. I have experienced kundalini flows so intense that my body shook for several minutes. This was Spirit Source clearing old and harmful energy from my chakras. Spiritual people around the world have practiced the kundalini experience for thousands of years.

Speaking in Tongues

Speaking in tongues is prayer language. It is thought to be the result of a Christian believer receiving the Holy Spirit. It is said to empower one to do "the Lord's work." This is misleading. I began speaking in tongues one month after my born-again experience. To clarify, although it is believed by Christians that the prayer language is a result of receiving the Holy Spirit, from an energy standpoint, it is actually your high self connecting to your past life experiences. After my born-again experience (reconnecting with the Prime Creator), the prayer language that I used to communicate with the Prime Creator was drawn from past life experiences. While doing so, I spoke in different languages, which is referred to as speaking in tongues. Our souls have had many lifetimes on earth, during many periods of time, practicing different spiritual beliefs. Dialects change from time to time because past lives have occurred in different areas of the world.

When speaking in tongues, my primary language is the language of my ancestral spirits. I've had lifetimes in many other places and belonged to many nationalities in other lifetimes; therefore, my prayer language changes based upon which ancestors I'm communicating with. I do not understand these languages otherwise. This is exclusive to speaking in tongues, which is known as xenoglossy. However, much of Christianity teaches this as glossolalia.

I've come to realize that was not accurate, because it wasn't communication with the Holy Spirit; I was drawing from past life experiences while communicating with the Prime Creator. As for spiritual experiences, I have had past lives as a monk, a nun, shaman, kahuna, priest, and an evangelist. I drew, and continue to draw from those past spiritual experiences to gain a stronger spiritual understanding and develop talents and abilities to help in my evolution as a spiritual being.

Tongues and Interpretation

If you are inclined to speak in tongues to a congregation in church, the words are a product of the collective consciousness. This is referred to as "tongues and interpretation." One person speaks an unknown language to the congregation and another person "interprets" the meaning. Generally there are only a few people who have this gift. The people who interpret are entirely influenced by the collective consciousness. Sometimes the Prime Creator will attempt to break through the collective consciousness to convey an important message; most of the time, it is misunderstood or smothered by church leadership.

Group Prophecy

Group prophecy occurs when an individual, usually during a worship service, speaks to a congregation or group of people with a message supposedly from the Holy Spirit. I would give prophesies in church services on a regular basis. When I felt the anointing, I would share the words that came to mind with the group. When the anointing stopped, I was finished speaking. Most of the time my message was influenced by the collective consciousness, and it was always a variance of the same message, which was encouraging yet generic in nature.

A valid question is whether the messages delivered during group prophecy are from the Prime Creator or made up from the collective consciousness of the church by the person sharing. The answer is that it can be both. It depends on the person sharing the prophecy. Most of the time, the message is from the collective consciousness of the group. The leadership of the group dictates the beliefs of the collective consciousness. Observe the prophecies from different churches. The prophecies are a reflection of the personality of the leadership, and each religious group has their own set of messages and beliefs that are based on that leadership's emphasis and doctrine.

My experience has been that the messages give false hope. Additionally, the messages can be so generic in nature they can be interpreted many ways. There are members of congregations that live just to hear prophecies, expect to hear something new and exciting, and will go to church to get their prophecy fix for the week. Occasionally a prophecy truly does benefit someone and bring him or her hope, especially if he or she is going through a particularly hard time. However, members can become disappointed if their expectations aren't met and the Spirit doesn't show up and give them a message. My interpretation is that the end result of group prophecy is a group consciousness dependent on illusions and full of false hope.

Consider a hamster on a wheel. Does it matter how fast it goes or how excited it gets? The hamster is still going around in circles, perhaps expecting to get somewhere, when really all it is doing is getting exercise. Although exercise is a good experience, my conclusion with twenty-five years of prophecy is that most of the time it does not produce much benefit except to get people excited and deliver false hope.

Personal Prophecy

There is also personal prophecy, which is a message given to a specific person by someone who is considered to have the gift of prophecy. Prophecy is a message from the Prime Creator to the gifted person. This can often keep members in the group, since the message is directed to one specific individual, and the motivation behind the prophecy is dictated by the group consciousness of the church and the intent of the leadership.

The purpose of the prophecy is to help the person understand the Holy Spirit's intent for the individual. It can be very difficult to determine whether the message is really from the Prime Creator or if it's a manipulation from the collective consciousness in order to persuade an individual to believe, act, or perform in a manner that is purely beneficial for the group rather than for the individual.

Laying On of Hands—Healing and Miracles

The laying on of hands has been used for thousands of years worldwide. I've been in many church services where people felt the so-called "anointing" that led them to pray for healing for others, and nothing happened. Time and time again, they'd repeat the process for different people with the same lack of results. They were simply stimulated by the collective consciousness of the group rather than by the Prime Creator.

Under the correct circumstances, laying on of hands will result in healing and miracles. This practice occurs when we place our hand on someone who needs healing, and we send energy from our chakras to them. I have laid hands on people and seen them healed. What is going on? I was told by the church, "It was the anointing of God that caused them to be healed." Not really!

Looking at this from a Christian standpoint, the terminology "anointing of God" refers to the power of the Prime Creator going to the healer. The "anointing" is what's supposed to heal. However, the anointing I'm referring to is tied to the group consciousness. What happened was that someone who had their hand on the person who needed healing had a connection with the Prime Creator and the energy flowed with enough power through them into the other person to manifest the healing.

The dynamics to consider regarding healing work include *desire* (a wish to create or accomplish something) to see the person heal, the *willingness* to use your energy for healing, and the *belief* (intent) that healing will occur. These factors allow the healing energy from the Prime Creator to manifest. The ability to manifest enough energy from the Prime Creator requires a clear channel for energy to flow from our chakras into the person we intend to heal. Angels and guardians are generally involved in the healing process as well.

Before I attempt to heal a person, I must *first ask for permission* (see the following section "Should Everyone Be Healed?") either from the individual or from the parents if he or she is an infant; I must ask their angels or guardians as well. I personally bring energy from the area above my crown chakra down my spine and into my spirit center. From my heart, or zero point, I manifest energy to the person. Other healers have different methods to channel energy for healing. There are many effective techniques for healing.

It is even more powerful when a group of people agree and focus their intent on healing. The power intensifies and the collective consciousness of the group creates efficient results. Note that hands don't necessarily have to touch the person; it is the transfer of energy that is important, and this can be conducted anywhere.

It is important to emphasize that *you must believe that your request will manifest* or you are wasting your time. Be sure to ask that the energy from the Prime Creator flows through you.

Should Everyone Be Healed?

Not everyone is supposed to be healed. Christians will often ask, "Is it God's will for this person to be healed?" To clarify, God's will is really your own souls' will. Our souls come to earth and decide when and where they will live and die. Whether we are conscious of it or not, our soul understands its purpose on earth.

It is difficult for some to accept the concept that not everyone should be healed. I know that I have the ability to heal, and I find it very difficult to back off. I have healed people from a variety of diseases and ailments; however, I have learned to ask for permission first. The law of relativity states that each soul has certain challenges to face while on earth. Our souls come to earth to experience various situations in order to spiritually learn and improve.

At times, healing occurs in stages rather than all at once. Partial or stage-by-stage healing allows the person to learn from the experience. *Each person and situation is different.* There are times when the soul is ready to depart, such as when it has completed its lessons or after it came to experience a particular event on earth. That is why it is so important to ask for permission. Otherwise, you could interrupt the person's purpose.

When a loved one passes, it can be more bearable and easier to cope when we remember that our souls have been here before and will continue to reincarnate until they are ready to move on. It can be difficult to watch someone suffer in pain from an illness. It may not make sense at the time, but there is a reason.

The law of cause and effect states that there is no such thing as chance or coincidence. *Everything happens for a reason.*

Yes, it can be difficult to understand, for example, why an infant dies prematurely, or a son or daughter is killed in military service, or a loved one dies in an auto accident before they had a chance to experience life. Remember, the soul is not dead. The spirit and consciousness of the deceased is in another dimension. The experience was necessary—even if we don't understand it. It may have been necessary for the soul to experience for its evolution or it may have taught us a lesson.

I have heard the question, "If God exists, then why did he allow my loved one to die? I thought God was supposed to be love." The answer is that God's love is a frequency of energy that allows all things to exist in harmony. We are all connected to the Prime Creator, and before we came to earth, we had a set plan for the soul. The Prime Creator does not decide our fate; our soul makes plans before arrival and controls our destiny.

Discernment of Spirits

Discernment of spirits and/or entities is the ability to recognize the type of spirit(s) that is manifested in an individual's life and/or surrounding environment. I have learned through practicing healing how to recognize and release spirits from people. I am able to recognize spirits while meditating in the fourth and fifth dimensions. The third eye is the psychic avenue by which spirits are recognized by sight (clairvoyance), sound (clairaudience), feeling (clairsentience), or a combination of the three.

Spirits/Entities

What is a spirit or entity? It is an energy form that manifests a consciousness and has the ability to perform certain activities. These terms are interchangeable; however, spirits and entities originate from various places.

Some religious groups believe that if an individual is struggling with a certain harmful behavioral problem, then it is due to some evil spirit. It can be, but in actuality it is usually not an evil spirit, but rather the low self in need of some discipline. The low self needs some training on how to behave and resist temptations associated with that particular behavior. The process of correcting the problem behavior involves the lower chakras and generally consists of clearing the energy patterns associated with that behavior. The high self and middle self are responsible for disciplining the low self.

My experience in energy work and healing has revealed that there are three levels of entities not associated with heavenly or evil spirits: high self, low self, and cross dimensional entities. It is possible for the entities to be souls (high or low) although this is fairly rare. It is more common for the entities to be high self or low self or cross dimensional. High and low self entities are energy forms from people's high and low selves that attach to other people. High and low souls are the souls of people who attach to other people's auras. Cross dimensional entities are energy forms that can come from different dimensions.

Before beginning, I always ask my angels if I have permission to help a person. Then I find out what kind of entities they have. If the individual has entities, I ask if I can expel them. If not, I will not work on the person. If I did I would risk picking up their entities, which could result in my own illness or death.

For example, a friend of mine who performs energy work helped a woman but did not check thoroughly to see if she had entities. He picked up an entity that was dwelling in her heart chakra, and he experienced intense physical reactions as a result. He came close to a heart attack and suffered for months under the influence of this entity. He lost touch with his energy work abilities as well. It took the help of another experienced energy worker to revive him. It is incredibly important to learn to dowse or consult with your angels before proceeding to help another.

Low Self/Soul and High Self/Soul

Entities from the low or high self/soul are from people whether alive or deceased. Energy from one person can transfer to another. Sometimes when a close friend or relative dies, their low or high soul energy attaches to another person's low or high soul. In this case, the relative will take on their personality. In another example, a person can take on low or high self energy (not to be confused with the soul, as it is energy from the other person). This is usually done when a person has had physical contact with another, or it can even occur through a phone conversation. The high or low soul is capable of splitting.

For example, it's possible for people to have a part of their mother's or father's soul in them while their parents are still alive. In many cases, I've needed to remove the low or high soul of relatives from someone I help so that the person can have clarity and think for himself or herself instead of being influenced by the soul of another. I ask the visiting soul to return to where it came from. This is discussed in detail later in the book. Here is an example regarding the high souls of relatives:

A woman came to me for help because she was in a state of confusion. I checked her for entities and discovered the souls of both her grandmothers, who had both passed on. The grandmothers' high souls had entered the woman's high self. This created a tremendous amount of confusion for the woman, especially in her third eye chakra. She seemed to always be in a state of confusion and struggled to make decisions, even ones as simple as selecting what to eat for breakfast. She had not only both of her grandmothers' souls influencing her, but her own high soul as well. No wonder making a decision was such a challenge! Once I crossed the souls over and helped them go to a higher dimension to be with their soul group, her mental clarity improved tremendously. She is now able to make decisions for herself and enjoy her own personality.

There are also some low self entities that attach to people and prompt them to conduct harmful or destructive behaviors. At times it can lead to violent or suicidal tendencies or to ill health. I have had to remove entities from a child who had been exposed to sexual abuse or pornography. These entities transferred from the person performing the act to the low, middle, and high selves of the exposed innocent child. Since the child didn't understand sexuality, the entity created an unsettling disruption for him. This resulted in the child crying for hours at a time and being unable to sleep. In this situation, the harmful entities had to be removed before healing and healthy development could occur.

Alcohol and drug users are especially susceptible to entities because while under the influence, their chakras are open to energy. Also, the more sensitive individuals are to energy, the more likely they are to allow energy to enter their aura. It's important to shield the aura on a daily basis to prevent susceptibility.

Cross Dimensional Entities

Cross dimensional entities can be destructive and harmful energy forms that may be picked up through watching movies or playing video games that are filled with excessive violence, horror, or anything that creates fear. Feeling fear and fear of the unknown usually cause a person to become susceptible to entities.

The energy that's generated from the movie creates a field of consciousness, and the subconscious mind cannot distinguish between reality and unreality. When there are feelings triggered, such as fear, the conscious mind accepts what it sees as reality, which allows the entity to remain. The energy from the entity is held in the chakras. An entity's presence usually manifests through nightmares and fear or anxiety.

I have removed cross dimensional entities from a person who was still experiencing fear days after she watched a disturbing movie. As I communicated with the entities, I asked where and why they had entered that person's aura. Their response was that they were attracted to the energy of the observer, and because of the observer's attraction toward the energy demonstrated, the observer opened herself up and the entity was able to enter the person's aura. Once in the aura, the entities continued to manifest the energy of fear. They were oblivious to the idea that this was causing problems within someone. To them, it was nothing more than a large energy field they were able to inhabit. I created a vortex and sent them back to their origin. After that, the person returned to normal.

Heavenly Spirits/Entities

Heavenly spirits/entities are energy forms that operate in higher dimensions to aid the development of humankind. They are our helpers, and we commonly refer to them as angelic beings or guardian angels. My experiences have led me to believe that every soul has an angel for protection, strength, and assistance. They operate in the fifth dimension or higher.

There are guardians that aid me with information. They are highly evolved beings that come from other galaxies to aid and provide information to the angels and humankind. There are also ascended masters, which are former humans whose souls have evolved to a very high state of consciousness. They also work with the angels and aid humans for healing and information.

Also, there are other helpers that are referred to as guides. Guides are souls that have previously lived on earth and have chosen to help humans instead of reincarnating. They operate in the fourth and fifth dimensions. They act as information gatherers and can warn us of current and future events. They are likened to being our shadow in the sense that wherever we are, they follow. They help us with our daily decisions, if we ask them. They are not all-knowing. They have a limited understanding; however, they are capable of gathering and providing useful information. My angels, ascended masters, guides, and guardians often aid me with information regarding healing and the future.

Devic Spirits

Devic spirits are energy forms from the Prime Creator that aid and maintain earth's balance. They help the plant and animal kingdoms and are commonly referred to as fairies or gnomes. Connected to Earth Mind, they operate at the devas level (knee chakra or second dimension). They are here to help the earth's balance and should not be confused with evil spirits. These energy forms can be felt through gardens and nature. Certain colors of plants attract certain devic spirits. For example, lavender, purple, and pink shades attract fairies. Trees and green plants attract gnomes. I've noticed reds, oranges, and yellows attract menehunes, as do trees and bushes.

Low Spirits of Earth Mind

Low spirits of Earth Mind are the low souls of people who choose not to reincarnate. When a low soul makes this decision, they are contained in Earth Mind and remain there. They are commonly referred to as our ancestor spirits. They are able to aid us in understanding our past life experiences as well as our physical talents and abilities. There are some cultures that understand this concept very well. I have learned to communicate with my ancestors often and love them dearly. They assist me while I'm helping others, and they protect me from destructive and harmful energy forms, especially while I'm helping other people.

Spirits of Darkness

Spirits of darkness operate on the opposite polarity from angels and guardians. They are energy forms that originate from and have chosen to operate in the lower regions of Earth Mind. Their intentions revolve around domination, control, and their own interests rather than the welfare of humankind, which is why they are considered evil. They lack regard for the needs or well-being of humans and will use them to fulfill their own interests. Evil spirits have the ability to manifest in different forms. Their energy comes from Earth Mind, and they also draw energy from fear in people.

When people are oppressed (influenced) by or possessed (fully controlled) by evil spirits, they lose their ability to think, reason, or act normally. While attempting to rid someone of an evil spirit, an understanding and concentrated power from the Prime Creator is required in order to release the person from spirit control. The afflicted individual must have the desire to be rid of the spirit, the strength to resist it, and the intent to never give it the opportunity to return.

Inexperienced individuals who engage in Ouija boards or what are considered occult practices (such as calling upon spirits of the dead) are especially susceptible. When they contact the spirits, they can be misled by the spirits telling them they are a deceased person, only later to discover the spirit simply wanted access to them. I refer to these spirits as deceiving spirits. The more you interact with these spirits, the more exposed you become. They can take your energy, which can result in illness. I strongly advise to stay away from Ouija boards. Nevertheless, despite lacking regard toward humankind and pursuing their own interests at any cost, they are vital for existence. The law of polarity states that there must be both positive and negative energy in order for matter to exist.

There is an imbalance on earth as there is more negative energy than positive. A strong attraction toward the dark side exists because it is glorified and portrayed as exciting by the entertainment world. This is understandable since we are usually attracted to things that are more powerful than ourselves and more exciting than the daily humdrum of life. However, lack of understanding about this type of energy can create problems for vulnerable individuals. Consider the law of attraction. What we attract is what we get. It's important to understand that this energy is very real and powerful, does not have your well-being in mind, and is usually more powerful than the average individual.

I have had to learn to set boundaries while working in Earth Mind. While I do explore past life experiences when helping others heal, I usually don't work below the midrange of Earth Mind. I mistakenly ventured past my usual boundaries into areas where I was unprepared, and I was attacked by energy from the evil side. I came close to dying before I was able to get rid of the energy. Fortunately my angels, guardians, ancestors, and friends who practice energy work came to my rescue. I thank the dark side for teaching me limitations and how to exercise caution.

I learned to use the frequency of love from the Prime Creator (a violet or white light) to protect my aura. Darkness is simply the absence of light, and light dissolves darkness. While the church is waiting for Jesus to return and defeat darkness, the reality is that the Prime Creator is available to aid humankind as a whole as we discover our individual power and use it to change the world. As more people learn to manifest this light of love, more of the darkness will fade.

Summary

- The anointing experience is a euphoric sensation that occurs when chakras are stimulated by surrounding energy from others. It is often misinterpreted as the Holy Spirit.
- The kundalini experience is the connection of positive and negative energy that repeatedly descends and ascends through our body as a flow.
- Prayer language results when the high self connects with past life experiences.
- Speaking in tongues (tongues and interpretation) during a religious congregation is the result of collective consciousness influence.
- Group prophecy occurs when an individual, usually during a worship service, speaks to a congregation or group of people and gives them a message supposedly

from the Holy Spirit. Generally, but not exclusively, this message is strongly influenced by the collective consciousness.

- The leadership of a group will dictate the beliefs of the collective consciousness. Each group has their own set of beliefs and messages based upon leadership emphasis and doctrine.

- Personal prophecy is a message given to a specific person by someone who is considered to have the gift of prophecy.

- Healing through lying on of hands occurs because a person has a connection with the Prime Creator and its healing energy flows through them and is directed toward another.

- There are three required factors for healing: desire, will, and intent (belief).

- Ask your angels for permission before attempting to heal someone, and ask if they have entities.

- Not everyone is supposed to be healed.

- God's will is actually your souls' will. God's love is a frequency of energy that allows all things to exist in harmony. Our souls control our destiny.

- Discernment of spirits is the ability to recognize types of manifested spirits.

- The third eye is the psychic avenue by which spirits are recognized by sight (clairvoyance), sound (clairaudience), feeling (clairsentience), or a combination of the three.

- A spirit or entity is an energy form that manifests a consciousness and has the ability to perform certain activities.
- The aura should be shielded daily to prevent entity and harmful energy susceptibility.
- There are three types of entities: low self, high self, and cross dimensional.
- A low self or high self entity is from another person (alive or deceased).
- Cross dimensional entities can be destructive and harmful energy forms usually picked up from the media.
- Heavenly spirits are energy forms from higher dimensions; they aid the development of humankind.
- Devic spirits are energy forms from the Prime Creator that aid and maintain earth's balance.
- Low spirits of Earth Mind are low souls that choose not to reincarnate.
- Spirits of darkness are energy forms that originate and operate in the lower regions of Earth Mind.

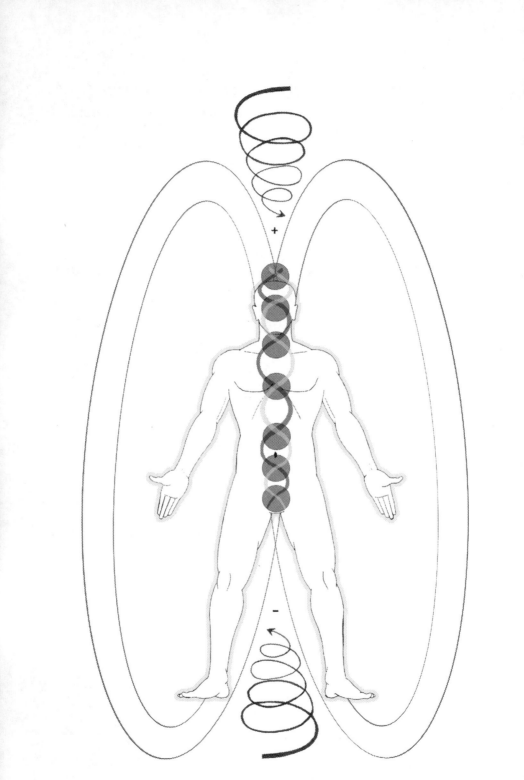

Kundalini Flow

PART 3

Ego, Self-Evaluation, and Clearing Techniques

CHAPTER 12

THE EGO AND THE DECISION TO CHANGE

Emotions are energy thought fields that vibrate within the chakras. Emotions accompany the beliefs that define us. This is the ego. The ego is the identity center connected to the entire chakra system, and it holds our intentions, such as who we are and who we want to be. It's located in the middle self, which helps govern the high and low selves.

In the next chapter your ego may be challenged. Here are a couple of questions to consider:

- What will I do if I decide that I may have been incorrect in my religious beliefs?
- Am I willing to admit that perhaps it is time for a change?

Whatever your response to these questions may be, remember that the choice is entirely yours. Will you allow your ego to get in the way? It may be a difficult decision to decide to change, because it will be life-changing for the soul. It may require significant changes in lifestyle and attitude. *It is your journey and you must decide for yourself.* Everyone has free will.

If change is desired, an evaluation of beliefs and associated emotions is required. Evaluation and change involve desire and will. Jesus Christ stated in the Lord's Prayer, "Let your will be done on earth as it is in heaven" (Matthew 6:10). Christianity has interpreted this to mean that in order to serve God, one must surrender the will to God. In reality, the will is not surrendered to God but to the church or religious group. *God's will is really your own souls' will.*

Some religions teach that a person cannot be spiritual unless the ego is completely emptied. I disagree! Without a balanced ego, the high soul does not have the opportunity to empower itself as a spiritual being capable of cocreating with the Prime Creator. Our souls exist to experience all things possible, and when we choose to reincarnate, the ego plays a vital role in survival and fulfilling our purpose on earth. The ego drives us toward necessary accomplishments and actions.

Ego balance is the greatest challenge to overcome in spirituality. The identity or ego of a religious group is based upon who they think they are and what they believe, which is vital for their existence. Religious groups follow the concept that the Word of God is infallible, so they strictly adhere to their set beliefs and disregard any contradictions. If someone disagrees with the church/group, it is a threat toward leadership ego. Disagreeing with or questioning scripture interpretations is considered a threat as well. Hard-core Christians may find it difficult to adjust their beliefs because their thoughts have been influenced by the premise that the Word of God is absolute truth.

Observation of the behavioral patterns of the collective consciousness of a religious group reveals a strong influence by leadership ego. For many years my purpose in life was centered on Jesus Christ, the church, and doing whatever I was told that supposedly pleased God. This collective consciousness convinced me that nothing was more important than this in life. Therefore, I completely understand how an individual can be devoted to their beliefs. Until the high soul decides it's time to change, an individual will hold the same beliefs—perhaps until his or her dying day. However, since you have made it this far into the book, perhaps your high soul is prompting you to reconsider your beliefs and/or discover your souls' purpose. Maybe it's time to release your beliefs and change your world.

Summary

- Emotions are energy thought fields that vibrate within the chakras and accompany the beliefs that define us.
- The ego is the identity center connected to the entire chakra system. It holds our intentions—such as who we are and who we want to be—that are located in the middle self.
- The ego plays a large role in the decisions we make.
- We have free will to make the decision to change ourselves.
- Our souls exist to experience all things possible, and when we choose to reincarnate, the ego plays a vital role in survival and fulfilling our purpose on earth.

CHAPTER 13

IDENTIFY YOUR BELIEFS

This chapter is intended to help identify beliefs that may be limiting your objectivity. Many of the thought patterns that the leadership of a church or group emphasizes are taught in such a way that it creates what I consider to be spiritual abuse. Many people leave churches emotionally scarred due to overzealous or ego-driven leaderships that leave people with little self-esteem. They experience guilt and condemnation for not measuring up to the standards put upon them or for questioning the leadership about their beliefs and behavior toward the congregation.

Let's examine some possible religious beliefs. They are separated into two categories according to the effect they play on emotions. Check the boxes of all of the beliefs you can relate to:

Fear-Based Beliefs:

☐ I am afraid that I am going to hell or not going to heaven if I leave the church.

☐ I am afraid that if I don't believe what the church teaches, I will go to hell.

☐ Homosexuality is sinful and condemned by God.

☐ It is sinful to question the pastor or the leadership of the church.

☐ When a person dies without being "born again," the soul goes to hell for eternity.

☐ Committing suicide is an unpardonable sin, and the soul will be punished in hell.

☐ If I don't speak in tongues, I am not saved.

☐ If I am not baptized in the church, I will not go to heaven.

☐ If I leave the church, something awful will happen to me.

Ego and/or Low Self-Worth:

☐ I have been an important person in the church. Where will I serve God if I leave?

☐ I am not good enough; I can't measure up enough for God to love me.

☐ God will not love me if I don't go to church anymore.

☐ I feel guilty if I don't go to church.

☐ I must ask the pastor's permission before I do something.

☐ The pastor/bishop/rabbi/guru/or priest is responsible for my soul.

☐ The church that I attend teaches that it is the only true church.

☐ Our church has more truth than all the others.

☐ The reason that God doesn't answer my prayers is because I have sinned.

☐ If I don't tithe to the church, then I don't love God.

☐ I am told not to associate with anyone who does not believe as I do.

☐ The husband has authority over the wife.

☐ The wife must do everything her husband tells her to do or she is in rebellion.

☐ If the wife disagrees with her husband or leadership of the church, she is rebellious.

☐ Women do not have authority to be in the leadership of the church.

☐ It is wrong to marry someone who does not believe the same as you do.

☐ It is wrong to marry someone of a different race or nationality.

These beliefs and many more may be found in the field of collective consciousness in front of the third eye chakra. You may hold only some of these beliefs and not all of them; you may also have some that are not listed here.

This book isn't just intended to help religious people. Even if you don't have a religious background, you can use a similar format to identify your beliefs concerning other matters that are controlling or highly influencing your life. Or perhaps in addition to your religious background, you may desire to reflect on other areas of your life as well. Since collective consciousness is what manipulates every culture or society, perhaps you can examine other aspects of your life to identify any needed changes, such as

• career/employment;
• education;
• military experience;

- personal interests (i.e., participation in sports, hobbies, recreational activities, etc.); or
- relationships.

The questions below are written in a format that allows you to insert the category you are focused on. You can use these questions for each category. Check all of the boxes you can relate to.

Fear-Based Beliefs:

☐ I am afraid to leave _____ because _____.

☐ I am willing to take the risk to make a change. (If not, why not?)

☐ I would be willing to make a change if I was shown how to be rid of certain controlling thoughts or beliefs. (If not, why not?)

☐ I'm afraid I won't be accepted or approved of by my peers, friends, or family without _____.

☐ I'm afraid of the financial outcome if I leave _____.

☐ I'm afraid I'll appear inadequate, weak, or pathetic if I chose to end my involvement with _____.

☐ What will people say or think of me if I leave?

☐ I feel I'm being forced into staying with/doing _____ in order to maintain my family's lifestyle or approval.

Ego-Based Beliefs:

☐ If I wasn't affiliated with _____, could I be satisfied with who I am as a person?

- ☐ Is my self-worth dependent on _____?
- ☐ My parents have certain expectations for me to live up to, but I'd like to exercise my own free will.
- ☐ I'm always told what I should or shouldn't do by _____. They make it hard for me to make my own decisions. Am I even capable of making my own decisions?

In following chapters we examine our emotions, associated energy, and how to release it.

Summary

- Many people leave religious groups emotionally scarred or with low self-esteem because of overzealous or ego-driven leadership.
- Many of our religious and other beliefs are fear or ego based and can be emotionally damaging.
- Religious beliefs, as well as many others are held in the collective consciousness in front of the third eye chakra.

CHAPTER 14

HOW TO CHANGE SELF-PERCEPTION AND BELIEFS

Once you decide you want to claim your rightful position as a spiritual being connected to the Prime Creator, the necessity will arise to release yourself of any false beliefs that control thought patterns. This is the way to gain personal power, become a cocreator with the Prime Creator, and be free of old thought patterns. Rather than believing you are a miserable sinner dependent on the church and its teachings, you can learn to manifest the power with the aid of the Prime Creator to bring love, happiness, and peace to yourself and others. Your soul can be free!

Making the Big Exit

Leaving any type of group—church, religious, or lifestyle (such as a career, relationship, etc.)—can be difficult and scary, especially if you've been involved for a long period of time, much like my experience. Some may need help leaving. If you feel that it's right for you to leave, the exercise provided below will help. Note that even if you have already left, the energy may still be in the chakras. When an individual has been subjected to a controlling group consciousness with a basis of fear, guilt, and uncertainty, paralysis may set in. Feelings of helplessness may occur, especially regarding change and moving on.

Recognize that your identity has belonged to a collective consciousness. Once you leave, you will have the power to take it back. Perhaps feelings of fear and doubt will surface when you decide it's time to leave. Remember, you have been instilled with many incorrect teachings that are not true, especially the belief that it is mandatory to go to church to be accepted by God. This is not true! *You are a part of the Prime Creator and are always loved. You were created in love and love sustains your spirit.*

Perhaps you will wonder what you will do next: What will become of me? What will people think about me? What will my family say and do to me?

These are normal and legitimate questions; however, they are all fear based. Perhaps a geographical move is in order, depending on your situation. In regards to what is taught about God—you have nothing to fear. Fear and guilt have been used by religious organizations for thousands of years to hold people in religious bondage, and it's nothing more than a control tactic.

You will know if and when it's the correct time to leave. You'll have run out of excuses and will be tired of listening to religious people tell you how to run your life. You always have the chance to be free. It takes courage and will, but you'll thank yourself in the future as you come to understand how to use your power to help yourself and others. It begins with desire.

You can personally revise the following statements to suit whatever area of your life you're focusing on (if it is not religion). When you are ready, read the following statements aloud. It's important to hear yourself say these words so that they register with your subconscious mind.

- "I have the *desire* to be free of religious control." (This demonstrates *desire*.)

It's important to hear yourself say these words so that it registers with your subconscious mind.

- "I *will* leave the church and find my own destiny for my soul." (This demonstrates *will*.)
- "I *will not allow* fear or anything else stop me from being free. I am free to do whatever I decide is best. I will do it now!" (This demonstrates *intent*.)

The goal is to believe that these statements have already occurred. Repeat them as many times as needed. The next step is to follow through with these affirmations through your actions.

Exercise 14.1   How to Release Undesirable Emotions—Energy Ball Technique

This technique is intended to assist in ridding anger, resentment, and other harmful or destructive emotions. It is designed to help clear emotions through verbal affirmations and pushing energy from the aura. You have the power to release any troubling emotions. Be sure you are alone in a quiet environment while practicing this technique.

Identify a troubling emotion. Focus on the emotion and feel it. For example, anger is usually stored in the stomach area. Take your awareness to the center of the head between the eyes. Close your eyes and bring your awareness back into your head as far as possible. (The purpose of bringing the awareness back is to disengage the frontal lobes and engage the subconscious mind.) Once your awareness is at the back of your head, place your hands out in front of your body and imagine that you are wrapping the emotion into a ball between your hands. Say aloud, "I release this energy from my subconscious mind and body. I will no longer hold or allow this energy inside me. I release it now." Push the ball away from you and imagine it floating away. Say, "I replace this with unconditional love. I am free to love." Refer to the illustration at the end of the chapter.

When energy is released, it must be replaced with new energy. It's important to make a positive affirmation after releasing the emotion. Before you begin the exercise, you can have a positive and encouraging replacement ready. Here are some examples:

- I will not hate anymore. I replace it with unconditional love.
- I will not be afraid anymore. I replace it with self-confidence and strength from the Prime Creator.
- I will not be dependent upon someone else to tell me what to do; rather, I will rely upon the inner knowing of my spirit and souls to guide my life.
- I will not be upset by critics. Instead, my self-esteem comes from the freedom I have as a spiritual being exercising my right to experience whatever I choose.

- I will no longer feel unworthy of God's love. I am learning to be a cocreator with the Prime Creator and learning to manifest unconditional love.
- I will not allow others' perception of my sexual preference and/or gender to keep me from reaching my full potential as a spiritual being, since the Prime Creator is comprised of both masculine and feminine polarity working in harmony.
- I release the fear and worry about going to hell. My spirit and souls are connected with the Prime Creator, and I will choose my path after death.
- I release the control of the church on my life. I take my power back and use it to become the spiritual being that I choose to become.

Whatever affirmations that you declare about yourself should be written down and repeated over and over until your subconscious mind believes what you say. The reason you believed what you previously did was due to the repeated messages you received from the group consciousness of the church. Your subconscious mind perceived it as truth.

Summary
- To regain your personal power, it is necessary to release some beliefs from your subconscious mind.
- You are part of the Prime Creator and are always loved. You were created in love and love sustains your spirit.
- You always have the chance to be free.

- Apply desire, will, and intent when you decide it's time to move on and adopt new beliefs.

- Use the technique provided to release undesirable emotions such as anger and resentment.

- Write down and repeatedly say aloud your declared affirmations.

Energy Ball Technique

CHAPTER 15

HOW TO RELEASE LOWER CHAKRA ENERGY

In this chapter we focus on the lower chakras and how to release harmful energy. Each chakra is connected with organs in the body. Energy affects health. There are several techniques available to clear chakras. This one is more advanced than the example in the preceding chapter. They are similar; however, this includes a meditation technique. The technique in the previous chapter can be used as an alternative to this one, if desired.

Root Chakra

Consider your religious experiences and direct your thoughts toward any relevant fears that come to mind. It is a good idea to write them down. You may only have time or energy to work on a few items at a time. Don't be in a hurry. It took months or even years to instill the beliefs connected to these emotions. You want to be as thorough as possible while clearing this harmful energy.

Here are some common fear-based concerns and thoughts associated with the root chakra:

- God will not love me if I leave the church.

- What are people going to say and do if or when I decide to leave?
- Will there be a reprisal from my family or people from church?
- Will I lose God's blessing since I am no longer giving the church money?
- Church attendance is mandatory for salvation.
- I have failed to measure up to God's standards.
- Will God allow me to become sick as punishment, or stay sick because he does not love me any longer?

The list just keeps going on and on because many religious beliefs were designed to control people, and religions have hundreds of years of experience in manipulating humankind. I recommend that you write down all of these things as they come to you, even after you have finished, just to remind yourself that you no longer are controlled by these thought patterns. Fear, selfishness, sickness, anxiety, health, security, abundance, giving, and fearlessness can exist within the root chakra. These thought patterns can apply to any aspect of our lives, such as careers, relationships, education, etc. The following exercise can be used for beliefs that don't involve religion. Simply substitute what is mentioned as religion with whatever topic you are working on.

Exercise 15.1   Meditation Technique for Clearing Root Chakra, Sacral Chakra

To begin the exercise, find a quiet place and turn off all electronic devices. Close your eyes and bring your awareness to the center of your forehead (between your eyes). Bring your awareness back in your head until you feel as though you might fall off the back of your head. Move your awareness down the spine as though riding an elevator. Pretend you are on level six. Imagine going down five levels to the bottom of the spine and stopping at level one. (If you are unable to visualize this then focus on the energy and associated emotions and pushing it out. Or, refer to the technique in the previous chapter.)

The door opens and you see a red circle of light. (Don't see light? That's okay; it's not cause for alarm and it's not necessary to see anything.) Identify the belief, thought, or emotion you wish to release. Imagine forming it into a ball of energy with your hands. Say, "I no longer allow this idea to exist within me and I release it now." Imagine pushing it away from you with force so that it leaves you permanently.

Here is an example:

The identified belief is, "Since I'm leaving the church, I'm afraid God will not love me anymore." To release this fear and belief and replace it say, "I no longer accept and believe that if I leave the church, God will stop loving me. I release this belief and fear from me [push the ball of energy away from your body] and replace it with the belief that I am loved by everything and everyone!"

Another example is the identified belief, "I'd like to change my career, but I'm afraid of being criticized or disowned by my family/peers." To release this fear and belief and replace it, say, "I have the freedom to experience my own life, and I no longer have the need to be under the control of my family. I have the power to choose for myself. I do this with acceptance for myself and unconditional love toward my family."

It's important to replace all of the harmful emotions and thoughts with new beneficial ones. If perhaps you are thinking this is a project, you may be right. However, your souls make it worth the effort. When you are finished clearing, you will be a different person, capable of exploring new ideas and concepts. Understanding of yourself and learning to work with the Prime Creator (and helpers of Spirit Source) will help you find new purpose in life. My wish for you is that you experience new joy and peace to help yourself and others live more meaningful lives.

Sacral Chakra

Take the elevator to level two. This is where our ability to express our sexuality and creativity exists. Here we find desire for reproduction and pleasure, lust, religious guilt, perversion, fantasy, or fixation of sexual pleasure. If you identify a belief, thought, or emotion that should be released, follow the exercise provided above in the root chakra section.

Homosexuality

I learned something about sexuality through the process of healing and clearing energy patterns from others. It has taken me a long time to reach an understanding regarding homosexual behavior. I have always been heterosexual, and religion taught and convinced me that homosexuality was due to a sinful, lustful heart. This is not true. Homosexuality is due to patterns of DNA. The devil has nothing to do with it. Our soul chooses when, where, and what it wants to experience on earth before arriving. If a soul desires to express itself as a homosexual, then it has the right and freedom to do so. The Prime Creator does not condemn this. The laws of the universe apply to everyone.

Low Self-Discipline

If you desire to live in a higher state of consciousness and connect with your high self, then discipline the low self and teach it how to control its urges. The low self has the maturity of a six-year-old. It does not have a conscience like the middle and high selves; it cannot distinguish between right and wrong. Our instincts exist here, as well as the desire for sexual gratification and satisfaction. This is why it's possible for people to have sexual partners without any personal connection—or perhaps without even knowing their name or story.

Lewd behavior and inappropriate sexual conduct are examples of undisciplined sacral chakra behavior. It is our responsibility to ensure that the high self teaches the low self appropriate behavior and discipline. This is accomplished through clearing and managing harmful sexual energy. (This can be performed through meditation.) Lust is an uncontrollable desire that goes beyond safe and respectful boundaries and can manifest into destructive or harmful behaviors. This isn't limited to sex. Lust can manifest in many ways, such as through greed, vanity, compulsive eating, etc. The devil doesn't cause lust. It is an undisciplined low self that allows inappropriate behavior.

We have an obligation to look out for the betterment of society. Knowingly spreading sexually transmitted diseases to others violates the laws of the universe. The law of oneness states that our energy is connected. The law of cause and effect states that manifesting destructive or harmful energy creates an imbalance on earth.

Sexual Partners

It doesn't matter if you went to church and became born-again. The energy from your sexual partners, past and present, remains in the sacral chakra. Although this may seem off topic from religious beliefs, the dynamics of sexual activity need to be addressed. This is especially important if you are struggling to get over a past relationship or are divorced. Refer to the exercise in the root chakra section. To rid yourself of unwanted sexual energy from past partners, take your awareness to the sacral chakra. Bring to mind the person(s) you were sexually involved with and say, "I do not want the energy of [insert name(s) if you can remember] to be in my chakra any longer." Take the energy and imagine that you roll it into a ball and push it away from your body as hard as possible. Say, "Leave me now and forever. I replace this energy with love and light."

You may find that you have beliefs regarding sexuality to replace as well. For example, "I feel guilty every time I have sex with my spouse." This can be released and replaced by saying, "I release the sexual energy from the past, and I am free to be a sexual person. I am sensual and I permit myself to enjoy this experience without guilt." Place the thought/belief into a ball and push it away from you as hard as possible.

Once the sacral chakra is completely clear, your conscience can decide what is appropriate and inappropriate. You have the freedom to choose your likes and dislikes. It is a personal decision so long as you respect yourself and your partners. What you decide to do influences the level the high self can operate. Find a balance that allows you to accomplish your souls' purpose.

These exercises need to be repeated for every person or experience that comes to the mind. This may take weeks or months. It doesn't have to be completed all in one sitting. Just work on it as time allows. Every time the exercise is performed, you should notice a release of energy from within. With each energy release it will become easier to maintain current relationships because there is less conflict of energies within the chakra. You will be freer to express your love in the present.

Summary
- It's important to release harmful energy from the chakras. Use the technique provided to clear your chakras.
- Write down your concerns and fears (for the root chakra) and sexual beliefs, guilt, or lingering sexual partner energy (for the sacral chakra) as they come to mind and work to release them as time allows.
- When harmful energy and beliefs are released from the chakra, they must be replaced with beneficial energy and beliefs.

- Our souls choose when, where, and what they will experience on earth before they arrive. The laws of the universe apply to everyone.
- It is our responsibility to ensure that the high self teaches the low self appropriate behavior and discipline. (This is accomplished through releasing and managing energy— perhaps through meditation.)
- Lust is an uncontrollable desire that goes beyond safe and respectful boundaries and can manifest as destructive or harmful behavior.
- We have an obligation to look out for the betterment of society.
- It's important to find a balance in your actions as that influences the level the high soul is able to operate and the souls' ability to accomplish its purpose.

Chapter 16

⋯⋯⋯⋯⋯⋯☀⋯⋯⋯⋯⋯⋯

How to Release Middle Chakra Energy

The Solar Plexus Chakra

This chakra is located in between the heart and the naval. This is where the middle self of consciousness is centered. This also is called the power chakra as it is the center of self-perception because our ego is situated here. Here in the solar plexus chakra, we find characteristics such as aggressive, dominating, abusive, authoritarian, and critical attitudes; lack of self-esteem; powerlessness; and inadequacy. The ego is connected with all of these behavioral characteristics. The goal is to have balance of personal power.

Exercise 16.1   Meditation Technique for Clearing the Solar Plexus Chakra

Close your eyes and take your awareness to the back of the head and then down the spine to the solar plexus chakra. You are starting at level six in the elevator at the third eye and going down to level three. The color associated with this chakra is yellow. If you do not see a yellow sphere of light, don't be alarmed. Just use your imagination and focus on the feelings that are associated with this chakra.

Before you start, it is helpful to make a list of the thoughts that you would like to be cleared. You can always come back to it and work on one at a time.

Here is an example: *self-perception of inadequacy, and failure to meet church standards.* This exercise can be applied to any aspect of your life where you feel inadequate or have concerns about failure.

Face the chakra and bring the belief to mind. Imagine wrapping it into a ball with your hands around it. Say, "The belief that I can't measure up to church standards is no longer allowed to exist in me." Push this energy ball away from your body as hard as possible. Try to visualize the ball of energy leaving. Say, "I no longer have to measure up to your standards! My soul is free to decide the standards that it will live by." Remember as you say this, you are not only replacing the old harmful energy but also reinforcing your subconscious mind.

You may have to repeat this process several times. Your vocabulary needs to reinforce the replacement. Listen to what you say and how you feel afterward as this is a good indication whether you are making progress. This is how you can check yourself to ensure that the harmful belief no longer exists. If you feel the old emotions, then use the technique again. Ideally your words and emotions will entirely reflect the new beneficial belief.

The Heart Chakra

The key thoughts and feelings associated with the heart chakra are in the areas of love and forgiveness. This chakra is located at the heart and referred to as the zero point in the human body. The color associated with this chakra is green. It is part of the middle self and stimulates the emotions. Here we find empathy, love, compassion, and understanding, as well as harmful items such as rejection, sorrow, despair, emptiness, and lack of love. Perhaps some of these feelings are associated with your religious experience. Again, you can apply the exercise to any aspect of your life.

Many times these harmful emotions are manifested through some kind of abuse, such as an unpleasant religious experience, and the energy will stay with people for the rest of their lives (unless cleared). Sometimes this emotional abuse is so powerful that a person will lose any inclination toward staying connected with anything associated with the concept of God or Spirit. Religious groups teach that sin separates us from God. There is no such thing! Regardless of our behavior, we are still connected spiritually with the Prime Creator. The law of divine oneness states that we are connected to all energy directly or indirectly on earth and in the universe.

I have worked with many women who have gone through emotional abuse from husbands or boyfriends. The energy of the spouse or boyfriend is still in their chakras, which reinforces the pain of abuse and resulting distrust. It also prohibits the person from moving on to a healthy, trusting relationship. Through the law of attraction, the women can attract the same type of partner again unless their chakras are cleared. They can use the technique described in this chapter to do so.

Exercise 16.2 Meditation Technique for Clearing the Heart Chakra

Close your eyes and take your awareness to the back of the head and down the spine to the heart. You are starting at level six (behind the third eye) and you will stop at level four. Face the heart chakra and focus. Look for a green sphere of light. For example, let's say you leave a religious group and since you no longer belong, you are rejected by your peers. Rejection can create emotions such as despair, sorrow, loneliness, and emptiness. These are the undesirable emotions to eliminate.

Since at the root of the emotions is rejection, the thought to focus and release is "rejection from family, friends, and church members." Take the thought and form it into a ball of energy and place your hands around it. Then say, "I dispel this emotion of rejection. I do not need anyone's approval. Leave me now and never return." Now push the ball away from you as hard as you can. Say, "I am accepted and loved by the Prime Creator."

When you are finished replacing all undesirable thought patterns associated with the heart chakra, it is always beneficial to ask Spirit Source for an abundance of love and light to fill your heart.

Let's practice another exercise to clear the undesirable emotions of abuse from someone close to you. Bring your awareness to your heart. Focus on the emotion of abuse and feelings associated with the abuser. Take the thoughts and feelings and form them into a ball of energy. Place your hands around the ball. Say, "I dispel this emotion of abuse from [name of abuser]. I will not allow your energy to remain in me any longer. I am pushing you out now. Leave me now and never return." Now push the ball away from you as hard as you can. Say, "I am now free from abuse and I am free to receive unconditional love from everyone and the universe."

You can do this exercise for any and all people you feel necessary.

Summary

- The solar plexus is also known as the power chakra because it is where the ego dwells. The goal is to have balance of personal power.
- Make a list of old or harmful beliefs that you wish to release and replace. Work on the list as time allows.
- Religious groups may teach that sin separates us from God. This is not true! You are always connected with the Prime Creator regardless of your behavior.

CHAPTER 17

·· ✳ ························

HOW TO RELEASE HIGHER CHAKRA ENERGY

The Throat Chakra

The throat chakra is located at the larynx and it is associated with the color blue. Since we eat and breathe through our throats, it is where we are nurtured both physically and spiritually. This chakra is part of the high self and is where we begin to connect to our higher consciousness. This is our communication center and where we manifest expression and receptivity. Harmful energy can create difficulty to express oneself and inhibitions, which can result in feeling unfulfilled, trapped, or smothered. Our vocabulary is an indication of these emotions. Love, peace, and joy are expressed here as well.

The effects of an unpleasant religious experience or any other experience can manifest a blockage in the throat chakra, creating a difficulty in expression. A prime example is the person who feels that they are not allowed to express their thoughts or feelings without being criticized or expelled from the church. So, this person learns to stuff the frustration inside even though they feel smothered, trapped, and misunderstood by the ones who are supposed to understand and love them. Even when they have had enough of the church and leave, they still carry that energy until it is cleared. This affects how they interact with people regardless if they are still in the church or not. It is important to clear the blockages so that we're able to express ourselves freely.

Exercise 17.1   Meditation Technique for Clearing the Throat Chakra

Close your eyes and take your awareness to the back of your head. Move down one chakra from level two to level three. Take your awareness to your throat chakra. This is an important chakra for emotional expression since it is the center for verbal communication. Look for a blue sphere of light. Identify the undesirable belief relating to expression and/or speaking (body language included) and its replacement.

Here is an example: "I have never been allowed to question the leadership of the church without being criticized or considered an unbeliever by the people of that church." Imagine forming this belief into a ball of energy between your hands. Say, "I have the authority and freedom to express myself any way I choose and question anything I choose. I release any inhibitions that do not allow me to exercise my thoughts and feelings. I release this energy from me forever. I am free to question anything I choose." Push the ball of energy away from you as hard as you can. Now feel the freedom in your throat.

You may need to go back to your heart chakra and release the anger that was associated with this type of bondage as well. *Some inhibitions affect several chakras, so don't hesitate to clear any chakra that you think holds the same patterns of energy.*

Again, it is a good idea to write a list of feelings that come to you and work through them one at a time. You may be surprised how many emotions have been suppressed.

The Third Eye Chakra

The third eye chakra is located between and behind the eyes. This is part of the high self, and it is located behind the indwelling soul. It's our focal point for thought patterns associated with energy involving our current life, past lives, and personality. Remember that you are learning to regain your power by exercising your *desire* to be rid of old patterns, your *willingness* to let go, and your *intention* to explore new ideas.

Sometimes we have developed a primary personality that is not beneficial, such as believing we are inferior to God and church leadership. You can use this technique to clear yourself of low self-esteem and regain your power. The reason for starting with low self-esteem is that you may have created a reality that is based upon your dependence for leadership guidance. This pertains to other areas outside of religion as well. We need to clear our mind's perception of who we have been so we can become the people we want to be. You are creating a new identity for yourself.

Exercise 17.2 Meditation Technique for Clearing the Third Eye Chakra

Close your eyes and take your awareness to the middle of your forehead. Move your awareness back as if you feel that you are going to fall off the back of your head. Look for a purple sphere of light. The clearer your third eye becomes, the better you will be able to see, feel, and hear energy.

Place the thought *low self-esteem* in a ball of energy and place it between your hands in front of you. Say, "Low self-esteem, your energy will leave me now and I no longer believe I'm inferior. I release this energy now. I am confident in myself and use my power to change." Push the ball of energy away from you very hard and imagine it leaving forever. Now is the time for you to start thinking about who you would like to be without the interference of religious persuasion.

Once you've completed this exercise, you can reuse it as necessary for any other beliefs or thoughts (anything you feel is inhibiting you from being the person you want to be). Chapters 18 and 19 also discuss the third eye and clearing techniques.

The Crown Chakra

The crown chakra is located at the top of the head and associated with the color violet. This is where we are connected to our higher consciousness. It is what I would refer to as the launching pad to the higher realms of consciousness, and it is the final holding area for thought patterns related to spiritual beliefs. If you're trying to clear yourself of old religious beliefs, you must be willing to let go of all past limiting spiritual beliefs.

If we have blockages in the lower chakras, we will not be able to access this higher chakra until they are cleared. This is a safety mechanism that protects us from what I would call "short-circuiting" ourselves. If harmful energy from low frequencies is allowed to rise up into this chakra, it will create an imbalance of polarity that could disturb us substantially. Before performing the exercise below, it is recommended you go through the exercises in chapters 18 and 19. It proves to be much more effective this way.

Exercise 17.3   Meditation Technique for Clearing the Crown Chakra

Close your eyes and bring your awareness to the center of your head. Pull your awareness back as though you are falling off the back of your head. Now raise your awareness to the top of your head. Create a ball of energy and place all undesired spiritual beliefs in it. Push it out in front of you and say, "I release all spiritual beliefs that do not serve my best interest, and I am free to explore new ideas for myself." Push the ball away from you hard, so it will never return to you. You must let go of the past if you are going to move into the future. Now you are free to formulate new ideas!

Summary

- The throat chakra is our communication center and where we manifest expression and receptivity. An unpleasant religious experience may manifest as a blockage in the throat chakra, which creates difficulty in expression. Use the meditation technique to release and replace any undesirable beliefs.
- Some beliefs affect several chakras. Clear any chakras that may hold the same beliefs and energy.

- Sometimes we develop a primary personality that isn't beneficial, such as believing we are inferior to God and religious group leadership. Use the meditation technique to release and replace these undesirable beliefs.
- To clear the crown chakra, you must be willing to release all past limiting spiritual beliefs.

CHAPTER 18

HOW TO REGAIN YOUR POWER

When you joined a religious group, it's very possible that you knowingly or unknowingly gave your power to them. This can also be applicable to other groups you've been involved with. This is an important technique to regain your power, even if you're uncertain whether you gave it over or not. The group still holds power over your subconscious mind.

Exercise 18.1   How to Regain Your Power

Find a quiet place where you will not be disturbed and turn off all electronics. Close your eyes and focus on the middle of the forehead. Bring your awareness to the back of your head and keep it there. You are now working in your third eye chakra. Focus your thoughts on the individual(s) that you gave your power to. There could be several leaders over the course of your life. Some examples are a pastor, bishop, priest, rabbi, guru, church board, or church council. Imagine you are standing in front of them (do this with one person at a time). Ask for your power back. Even though they had no right to take it from you, nonetheless, you handed it over when you acknowledged them as your spiritual advisor, perhaps recited vows, or allowed them to tell you what to do with your life.

Say, "I want my power back. Take back the precepts, teachings, guilt, and control you once had over me. You no longer have power over me." Imagine the spiritual advisor saying to you, "I give your power back."

You're done! Your subconscious mind is free to make its own decisions now.

No matter how peculiar this exercise may feel or seem, the law of divine oneness states that we are all connected to each other directly or indirectly by energy.

I have the ability to project my consciousness to any religious leader necessary in order to assist someone who is attempting to reclaim their power. I communicate with the subconscious of the spiritual advisors, and despite the egotistical demeanor and their belief that they can tell you what to do, the leaders always give the power back to whomever requests it. They know they didn't have any spiritual authority over anyone in the first place.

This exercise is important because it allows the subconscious mind to recognize that it's once again in control. It can be used for any situation in your life where you felt you gave your power to someone else. Now you know the truth that you can reclaim your power, and now that you have your power you are free!

> Then you will know the truth and the truth will set you free. (John 8:32)

Summary

- It's possible that you gave your power over to a religious or another type of group. The group will continue to hold power over your subconscious mind until you release the energy. Use the exercise to regain your power and allow your subconscious mind to recognize that it is once again in control.

CHAPTER 19

CLEARING COLLECTIVE CONSCIOUSNESS

When I am helping others free their minds of collective consciousness, I see the energy field in front of their third eye chakra that holds thoughts and beliefs concerning their religious experiences. Please refer to the "Collective Consciousness and High Soul" illustration in chapter 8. The energy field is cylindrical in form. Try and picture a CD or writable disk of sorts. Written on it is everything that you believe, such as spiritual ideas, doctrines, and the associated emotions that resonate within chakras. This technique is intended to help you clear religious beliefs associated with collective consciousness. This exercise requires concentration and imagination. Not everyone is able to use this technique effectively, but you should at least give it a try, and if at first you don't succeed, try again.

Exercise 19.1   Technique for Clearing Collective Consciousness

Find a quiet place where you will be undisturbed. Before beginning the following technique, read the below statements aloud to reinforce your desire, will, and intent to change your beliefs:

I desire to have clarity of mind to establish new ideas. I will not allow this spiritual energy of the past to remain in my mind any longer. I bring the light of Spirit Source down with power to dissolve this energy field that has controlled me. I no longer allow it to exist in me! I am now free to explore new thoughts.

You are exercising your power to be free. Repeat these affirmations several times before performing the exercise below.

Close your eyes and bring your attention to the middle of the forehead. Imagine pulling your awareness back in your head (in the same way as the previous techniques). Focus your awareness in front of your third eye and hold it there. You might see a circle of purple energy revolving around. This is your third eye chakra. Move forward through the third eye to see a swirling mass of energy. Imagine that there is a revolving disk of energy in front of you with all the beliefs that you have ever been taught regarding your religious beliefs written on it. This is the energy field that has blocked your freedom of thought as well as your soul from experiencing new things.

In your mind's eye, look upward and imagine an angel bringing a white light down from Spirit Source. Ask the light to come into the back of your head and visualize the light coming in and directed forward through the third eye into the energy field in front of you. You may see the light in a swirling vortex emptying out the energy field, or you may not see anything at all. If you don't see anything, just imagine and believe that it is taking place.

After you've done this, bring your awareness forward to just behind your eyes. Open your eyes. Think of religious beliefs. If your mind draws a blank, then you have succeeded in emptying your old beliefs. If you try and read the Bible, it may be as though you've never read it before. It may not make the same sense it once did now that the collective consciousness isn't controlling your mind. Once this technique is completed, you should be free to begin formulating new ideas!

The exercise for clearing the crown chakra should be repeated once this exercise is completed. There isn't a revolving disk of memory in the crown chakra, but there may be ideas that you are still holding on to regarding your former religious beliefs. Place the ideas in a ball and push them out from you. It is important to clear in front of the third eye using the technique described above as well as the crown chakra as described in chapter 17.

As I was learning how to do this technique, it was important to state the affirmations listed in the first part of the chapter because I truly wanted to clear my mind of all religious beliefs and start over. I wanted to formulate my beliefs based upon what my spirit and souls confirmed and agreed upon.

After I cleared the energy field, I literally took the Bible and began reading familiar scriptures that I had studied for over twenty-five years. I could not accept these scriptures as absolute truth because they did not resonate with my spirit and souls. Therefore, I started to use my meditation techniques to communicate with Spirit Source to gather information concerning spirituality. As I helped other people through healing, clearing entities, and crossing over souls, Spirit Source helped me formulate different beliefs concerning my spirit, souls, and afterlife.

I believe as I continue my journey, I will discover more and maybe even different information that will help me understand the meaning of life and how I can help other people. The old expression, "'school's out," meaning you're done learning, doesn't ever apply to our personal development. In your endeavor to gain greater understanding and more clarity, it may be necessary to clear out the old beliefs so that you're capable of objectively formulating new ideas. If some of the old ideas are still valid, then of course, you can maintain them. However, if something is no longer valid, or you no longer hold it to be true, you have the ability to let it go.

Summary

- Thoughts and beliefs related to spiritual experiences are stored in the collective consciousness located in front of the soul and third eye.
- Use the techniques provided to clear the collective consciousness. This allows you to begin formulating new ideas.

CHAPTER 20

BINDING AND LOOSING ENERGY

Our words have tremendous power. The old saying, "Sticks and stones may break my bones, but words will never hurt me" is false. The intention behind words is incredibly important because they manifest energy fields of thought that can bring extreme consequences. The concept of how words can be used to manifest intent with significant consequences is conveyed in this scripture:

> Jesus said to Peter, "I will give you the keys of the
> kingdom of heaven; whatever you bind on earth will
> be bound in heaven, and whatever you loose on earth
> will be loosed in heaven." (Matthew 16:19)

Jesus is saying that the intent of words manifests from oneself to others. Binding means that when a person makes a proclamation, they are manifesting/creating intent, which remains within the person as well as connected energy fields. Through the law of cause and effect, we are held accountable. Binding involves negative or positive energy from at least one individual. For example, when two people exchange wedding vows, they manifest intent not just to each other but to the universe as well. The same concept applies to the scriptural terminology known as loosing energy. When the time comes to release an undesirable intent, belief, or thought, the energy is "loosed."

Cords and Attachments

We attract others with like energy. It's easy to see how a group of religious individuals who share common ideas and desires are bonded together. To be bonded means to exchange energy with one another and have a cord of attachment. The term is also referred to as "cords of attachment," "attachments of energy," or "binding of energy." Bonding can occur between two people or within groups, such as a congregation. The law of oneness states we are all connected to one another. We can purposely or unknowingly connect to others just by agreeing to something, and we will be affected by the energy of the other people. The body's energy field can be affected by the negative and positive energy of whomever you are associated with.

We can also have cords attached from persons, places, and things. Places and things involve the energy field manifested in Earth Mind that we are connected with. Examples are homes, the city in which you live, the schools you are attending or have attended, or an object you care about. This can be beneficial or destructive, depending on its energy. You have the power to choose if you want to accept it or release (loose) it.

I recall in church, together as a congregation, praying and requesting the Lord to bind us together and join us all as one. This prayer was usually conducted while everyone held hands.

Sometimes we would sing songs with the same request. At first this scenario may sound lovey-dovey and grand; however, if you prayed this in church, you attached yourself to the positive and negative energy of everyone in the group. You gave more of your power over to the collective consciousness, and you would not be free to move on until you cleared yourself of it. Also, cords involving harmful energy can result in physical and emotional symptoms such as anxiety, depression, sleeplessness, insecurity, confusion, suicide, etc., which is another great reason to rid yourself of them.

If you have been treated unfairly by a group or individual and have made a conscious effort to forgive them, but the harmful emotions produced from the unfair treatment linger on and on, then forgiveness is not enough. The solution is to clear their energy from your aura. Try the energy ball technique provided in chapter 14, and if that does not work, then refer to the section below on energy cords.

Cords

If the energy ball technique did not eliminate undesirable energy, then chances are you are attached by an energy cord. This can be the reason why some people are ridden with guilt toward themselves—they still harbor feelings of anger and resentment toward a specific person even though they have repeatedly said they've forgiven them. They may feel condemned and have no joy. It's as though every time the name comes up, they experience anger and resentment, even though they don't want to anymore. If you feel it's time to set yourself free, try the technique provided below.

Exercise 20.1   Clearing Cords

This is a difficult technique and will require assistance from an experienced individual or from your spiritual helpers (i.e., angels or guardians). If you find that you are unsuccessful with this technique, please seek out an energy healer to assist. There will be a noticeable improvement in your energy level if this exercise is performed correctly.

It can be helpful to make a list of people from your associations that you may still be attached to. A person who is divorced may desire to clear himself or herself of the previous spouse. It can be difficult to find a meaningful relationship with someone new if the old energy from the previous spouse remains. The list doesn't have to be just the people you carry hard feelings for. It can simply be acquaintances that you no longer wish to be connected with.

If you believe you have cords attached and do not know who they are from, you will need the help of someone who has the ability to identify them. If you realize you have a cord attached to someone, and you want to continue to associate with them, that is your right to allow it to remain. Just because you disconnect the cord does not mean that you will not have physical contact with the person anymore. It means you do not have an energy connection with the person, and you can shield your aura to keep the person's energy from you. Remember, the purpose of disconnecting the cord is so that the person is not using your energy anymore. Please refer to the illustration, "Cord Attachments," located at the end of the chapter.

Begin the exercise by asking your angels or guardians for assistance to help you be rid of the unnecessary cords that are draining your energy (or have the person helping you ask). Close your eyes and bring your awareness to the back of your third eye. Think of the person you wish to release and imagine you can feel their energy. Visualize a cord connected from them to the back of your spine. Ask your angels or guardians to remove the cord of the person [insert their name] and thank Spirit Source for freeing you of the energy. Imagine the cord is taken out of your spine. Repeat this for every person on your list.

Some people report feeling a removal from their spine, while others feel nothing. If this technique worked, you will notice an improvement in your energy level immediately. You may feel a whole group of muscles relax in your back or shoulders. I had a cord attached to someone, and the left side of my shoulder was frozen up. After I released the cord, it took a little bit of time for the muscles to balance out again. A good massage will help move along the healing process.

Summary

- Intention manifests into energy forms with significant impact or consequences.
- Binding is the concept that a proclamation or declared statement remains within a person as well as connected energy fields.
- Loosing is the concept of releasing undesirable intent, beliefs, or energy, such as a bound proclamation or declared statement.

- To be bonded means to have an attachment to another person through the exchange of energy. This is also referred to as cords of attachment, attachments of energy, or binding of energy.
- Use the energy ball technique in chapter 14 to clear yourself of bound statements and/or bonds. If this technique is unsuccessful, try the energy cords technique. Make a list of people you think you still have an energy connection with to reference as you use this technique.

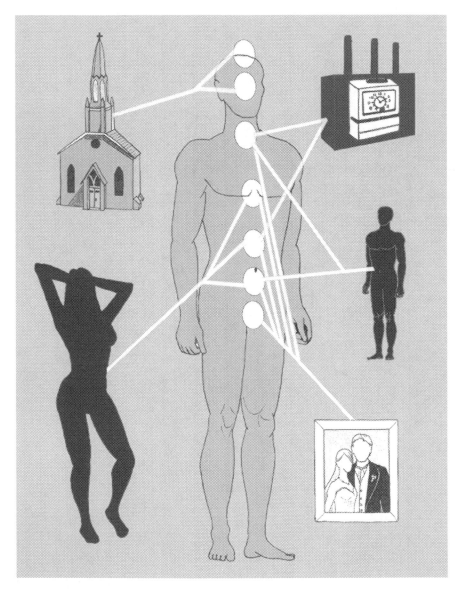

Cord Attachments

PART 4

Meditation, Prayer, and Spirituality

CHAPTER 21

MEDITATION AND PRAYER

Communicating with Our High Self

Now that you have had some practice with clearing your chakras, let's practice connecting to our high self with Spirit Source (referring to helpers from the Prime Creator). This should be your personal time for yourself. There are as many methods of meditating as there are golf swings. The main idea is to connect with Spirit Source and stay in the game. The game is discovering your emotions and how to control them, your personal desires and purpose on earth, and what you want to accomplish for yourself and contribute to humankind. You may have discovered some of these answers through your religious experiences. If so, use learned beneficial aspects and add to it as you discover more. Frank Jordan has a saying that I agree with: *"We learn what we want to become by experiencing what we do not want to be."*

Exercise 21.1   Meditation

This is a method of meditating that I use almost on a daily basis to receive information. Begin with a simple chakra clearing with spoons or crystals (see chapter 5). Pointed quartz crystals work better than spoons. Just point them in the same direction that you would spoons. To clear my chakras, I use a pair of smoky quartz crystals that I have programmed.

After you have finished clearing the chakras, place the spoons or crystals facing inward on your lap. This directs new energy into your chakras. Close your eyes and bring your awareness to the center of your head. Now pull your awareness back into your head as if you are looking forward from the back of your head. What you are doing is disconnecting your thoughts from the frontal lobes and directing your focus to the third eye chakra. Clear your mind and rest. Take slow, deep, and relaxing breaths. This will calm your mind and body.

Since your awareness is now centered behind the third eye chakra, go down each chakra and clear any dark, dense, or perhaps resistant energy that blocks the flow of new energy. Create a ball of energy and release it.

The idea in this meditation is to clear your mind to a point where it's possible to communicate with your high soul and Spirit Source. This is the perfect time to communicate with your high soul and find out what it desires. I've found that my high soul rests in front of my third eye. It is as if I'm speaking to myself when we communicate. It will direct me as to what it wants to do.

Proceed to go up to the crown chakra. Expand your awareness outward and upward. Imagine you are filling a room with your expanded energy. Try and feel the energy around you as you expand upward. Keep taking your awareness upward as if you are floating up into higher levels. You can imagine that you are on an elevator in a skyscraper going up to the top floor.

When you reach the penthouse, you will meet your angels or guardians. Your intentions need to be clear and your mind receptive to information. As your awareness expands upward, you are raising your vibration to a higher frequency.

When you feel as though you're finished for the moment, or you have reached the desired octave of frequency and contacted whatever helpers you desire and received the information you wanted, it will be time to return to the third dimension. Take your awareness down. Follow the octaves down. You may feel each dimension as heavier energy than the previous. Continue down into the third eye chakra. Take your awareness forward into your eyes. Open your eyes.

It is necessary to clear the energy from your meditation session or clear the energy of the person you assisted (if you are working with another person) from you. After you open your eyes, just simply take the energy of the person or place in your hands and push it out in front of you to clear it out. Otherwise you may find yourself mentally foggy for hours afterward because you're still holding on to the energy from your meditation or the person you were helping. I've found that after a long period of meditation, a swim in the ocean can ground my chakras so that I can concentrate on activities. I recommend you find some way to ground yourself after meditations such as these. You can use the grounding technique provided in this book.

There are twelve octaves of frequency in each dimension, so I start at the root chakra and count it as number one and go up the chakras, counting each one until I reach the twelfth, which is I AM. Then I expand my awareness upward to the next dimension (fourth). You will find yourself able to raise your vibration to higher octaves as you learn to clear your lower chakras of energy patterns that block a free flow of kundalini energy.

The practice of counting octaves is helpful to measure your progress. I find it gives me a reference as to which frequency level to access to contact my helpers. For example, if I'm going to contact the low souls of people, I can generally find them in the midrange of the fourth dimension. If I'm going to work with angels, I will work between the midrange of the fifth and sixth dimensions. If I'm going to work with ascended masters, I work in the sixth dimension. Ascended masters and angels generally work together. If I'm going to work with the guardians, I work in the middle range of the fifth dimension and higher. If I'm going to work with the assistants of the guardians, I must reach into the seventh dimension.

The practice of counting the octaves is a method I find very helpful. As I begin to read the energy of other people, I can focus on their energy fields and locate in which octave they're resonating. This is likened to an energetic pulse rate. The rate can fluctuate depending on emotions.

For example, if a person is going through a hardship, they will resonate in their root, sacral, and solar plexus regions. Another example is a mother nurturing a newborn. She may resonate in the heart and throat chakras because she is most likely expressing high amounts of love to her baby while nurturing. Everyone has an average frequency of vibration. It's based upon their level of balance between their own low, middle, and high selves. I find identifying where they are resonating helpful in order to gauge their level of progress.

Here is my personal process for this technique. It will be a different experience for everyone. As I reach upward, I am still in the third dimension until I reach the twelfth octave, the I AM chakra. At this point I see a light and hear a voice say, "Yes?" (as though I am asking, "What can I do for you?"). My high self directs me to the correct and necessary dimension to receive direction from Spirit Source. We have access to the lateral planes of consciousness (parallel lines of energy that flow throughout the world) in the fourth dimension so we can connect to the energy fields of the world. This is where psychic manifestation occurs (projecting intent to accomplish the tasks we set out to perform, such as communication with consciousness of others and healing).

Above the twelve octaves of the fourth dimension is the fifth dimension, which expands more into the universe, allowing me to manifest and gather new information from the universal consciousness of the Prime Creator. This is an open energy field that expands upward, rather than running parallel as is the case with the fourth dimension. The fifth dimension (and higher dimensions) holds information regarding the universe and future. I personally refer to it as universal consciousness of the Prime Creator. Also, these higher dimensions are where I listen to and receive new information from angels, guardians, and ascended masters.

The Difference between Meditation and Prayer

The difference between meditation and prayer is that prayer is making a request and/or expressing thanks to the Prime Creator. Meditation is listening (gathering information) and manifesting desire, will, and intent. When I am helping someone for healing or clearing their energy fields, I am soliciting prayer by asking for assistance from Spirit Source, and meditation by using my abilities to manifest the results.

This is why I say we are cocreators with the Prime Creator. There are times when I reflect back on my accomplishments and thank all the helpers involved, such as Gaia, ancestor spirits, devic spirits, guides, angels, guardians, ascended masters, and the Prime Creator. By working in harmony and love, we can change our world into a better place as well as change ourselves into better persons.

Exercise 21.2   Meditation and Prayer

Let's practice a combination of both prayer and meditation. Think of something that you need help with. Sit in a quiet place and if you have your crystals handy, place them both on your lap facing to the right. This can help you clear your mind and focus your thoughts on what you desire. Ask Spirit Source for guidance. Explain your situation and desires to your angels. Sometimes your deceased loved ones might be there to listen and comfort as well. Take some calming breaths, relax, and understand you're heard and accepted with unconditional love by the Prime Creator.

Some people have the ability to hear an inner voice respond, while some do not. You may feel in your heart a comforting energy flow of love, or perhaps nothing at all. Don't worry. Be patient. You are not alone and your requests have been heard. Spirit Source will direct you as to what you may need to do. There are many ways that answers may come to you. I have had angels speak to my inner voice or wake me up in the middle of the night to show me something I needed to do or know. I've had dreams and visions, and ideas from reading books; I've met people who have helped me. I have gone to some location and discovered the answer when I connected to the energy of Earth Mind. The list goes on and on.

Be open to receive the answer you are looking for, wherever you might be. The answer will come at the correct time for your soul. The law of divine oneness states that our energy is connected to everything and everyone, so Spirit Source will provide help for us in the best appropriate manner. Ask and you will receive. The law of cause and effect states that nothing happens to us by chance; there is always a reason for everything.

Jesus' Example of How to Pray

> Jesus said, "This is how you should pray: 'Our father in heaven, hallowed be your name. Your kingdom come, your will be done, on earth as it is in heaven. Give us today our daily bread. Forgive us our debts, as we also have forgiven our debtors and lead us not into temptation, but deliver us from the evil one.

'For if you forgive men when they sin against you, your heavenly Father will also forgive you. But if you do not forgive men their sins, your Father will not forgive your sins.'" (Matthew 6:9–15, The Lord's Prayer)

This is a classic Bible scripture—Jesus prays. See how many universal laws you can find within the scripture. This is my interpretation of how the prayer could be written according to the universal laws:

I recognize and respect the Supreme Prime Creator of the universe. Let its kingdom or desires reign in my heart so the will of the Prime Creator centered in love will manifest in the universe and on earth as well. Continue to provide for me the energy that I need to sustain life and to be prosperous. I understand the law of cause and effect; therefore, I have forgiven all who have taken advantage of me. Let your light fill and surround my aura so darkness cannot affect me and keep your angels and guardians around me for protection. Thank you for your assistance.

Exercise 21.3 Manifesting through Meditation

The following exercise can help you if you have prayed and received direction that requires your energy to manifest something in particular. For example, let's say that you are looking for a good place of employment. Spirit Source is opening up opportunities for you to find employment. Find a quiet place and begin the meditation technique by pulling your awareness back in your head behind your third eye. Make sure your chakras are clear. You don't want any distractions. Take your awareness down to the heart chakra. This is the zero point where all things are manifested.

If you have crystals, place one crystal in your left hand and place it on the left side of your body at the hip. Point it forward, parallel to the ground. Place the other crystal in your right hand and point the crystal inward at heart level, also parallel to the ground. You are now directing standing waves of energy from the past (left-hand crystal) to the present and the standing waves of the future (right-hand crystal) into the present.

Think of what you'd like to manifest and project the thought into the center of your heart. Holding on to that thought, take the crystals and place the right hand facing down under the chin and point the left hand crystal to face upward from the groin (both parallel to body). You are now pulling positive energy down from Spirit Source, which is the masculine positive energy that creates. You are pulling up female energy from Earth Mind that holds the form of the creation. Direct both of these energies into the zero point in the heart chakra. You now have positive and negative polarity manifesting the intent, and the standing waves of the present manifesting into form.

Imagine that you form your desire into a ball of energy and release it in front of you. Direct your intent into it and tell it to sustain itself and remain in form. Then believe that it is accomplished. Now the universe has the energy to answer your desire. Expect results. Remember the law of action—after this exercise, follow through with whatever physical action is required of you and experience the results. (For example, if you are contacted for an interview for the job you want, go to the interview!)

How I Manifest Healing Energy

I will describe the method of meditation I use for healing in hopes that it may benefit you. Feel free to adopt some or all of the things I do. To begin this technique, I take my awareness to the third eye and bring it back as though I'm going to fall off the back of my head. I go up and down my chakras and clear them. Once I know I have a clear channel from Earth Mind to my high self, I go down to Earth Mind and ask for help from Gaia and my ancestor spirits. I go up to my high self and contact my angels and guardians and explain that I'd like to help someone and how I'd like to help them.

Once I hear the angels and guardians respond that I have permission to work on the person, I dowse the person to see if I need to remove entities. (If you would like to learn more about dowsing, more information is available in Frank Jordan's book, *Clearing the Way*, pages 42–43.) If so, I speak to the entities and send them away to their sources of origin. I will continue to dowse the person until I know it's okay to proceed to work on them. Then I take my awareness to my heart chakra and expand it into the other person whom I'm working on. It doesn't matter if I'm physically with them or not. I connect to their energy and project my consciousness to their heart chakra. I connect to their subconscious mind and I hear them acknowledge me in their thoughts.

Then I go to each chakra, read the emotional energy, and clear the chakras. I do this by creating a vortex (referred to by Frank Jordan as vibra ports) on each side of the chakra to release harmful energy. I watch the dark energy release until I see the color of their chakras, now clear of dense harmful energy.

Next, I go to the location in the person's body that needs healing. I manifest healing from my heart chakra. There is where I'm guided by angels and guardians as to how to send energy to specific organs, vertebrates, blood vessels, cells, etc. Sometimes I see the body part being healed and vortexes of energy from Gaia and Spirit Source going up and down the person, healing their body. Everyone is different. I create the standing waves of intent for healing and send them to the person.

My helpers aid in the manner in which the energy is used to heal the person. Remember, we are cocreators with Prime Creator, and we have tremendous power available to manifest whatever we desire. When I am told by the angels that the healing is done, I expect good results and thank my helpers. I pull my awareness back from the person to my heart chakra. I release their energy from me by pushing it back to the person. I take my awareness back to my third eye and bring it forward to my eyes. I open my eyes.

I will wait to hear from the person I worked on. Sometimes it takes several hours or so for the person to feel the changes. I never advise anyone to stop taking medications. I advise him or her to go see the doctor. Sometimes the doctors cannot find any more symptoms or the condition and have no explanation for the patient. That's fine; the person is healed!

Summary

- At times we learn what we want to become by experiencing what we do not want to become.
- Try the meditation technique to connect your high self to Spirit Source. Begin by clearing the chakras.
- Universal consciousness of the Prime Creator (fifth dimension and higher) holds information regarding the universe and future.
- The difference between prayer and meditation is that prayer is asking, and meditation is listening. If you need clarity on a topic, just ask Spirit Source to help you—then listen.
- It is possible to manifest your desires or needs through meditation.
- Spirit Source will provide help in an appropriate manner specifically for you.

CHAPTER 22

PAST LIVES AND KARMA

The akashic records of Earth Mind hold recorded history of all our past lives. Our low soul/self is influenced by our past life experiences. The lessons that we need to experience on our evolutionary journey will continue to manifest with patterns or types of behavior until we recognize and master them. Some examples include learning consideration and compassion toward others and overcoming fears or phobias like fire, heights, water, darkness, etc. The list goes on and on because we have experienced many lifetimes.

When I work with others and help them clear past lives, I usually take one pattern or type of behavior that they're struggling with, such as anger, and try to discover as many lifetimes that deal with that same energy. I use my dowser to discover how many past lives pertain to that certain theme. Karma is the reoccurring energy from an experience that is either beneficial or harmful to us or others. Some people use their angels to help them discover and clear their past lives. The goal is to eliminate past karma that has created disturbing challenges for us in our lives so that we can have fulfilling and abundant lives.

One of the classic examples of karma is in the area of relationships. I've worked with many people, married or not, that have had several partners. They seem to go from one uneventful relationship to another, and when I take a deeper look, it usually follows a mother-daughter or father-son past life pattern. Another common past-life theme that creates disturbing relationships is when someone is mistreated by their spouse in a way that caused humiliation or some sort of grief. In many cases it's through adultery. In their next lifetime, the spouse reversed roles with that person and they experience the same situation again. The pattern continues to the next reincarnation. The karmic flow continues up to the present time.

When clearing the past lives, I go into the standing waves of time to that situation where the flow began, and I correct it so that the energy doesn't continue forward. The karmic flow changes once it is changed to unconditional love expressing itself for the well-being of all. People, here in their present lifetime, can decide whether they want to continue in the same old pattern. Now they have the opportunity and awareness to change, because they aren't influenced by that old energy anymore. They have the power to change their lives. The choice is still theirs.

Exercise 22.1 Technique for Clearing Past Lives

If you've discovered a karmic flow while meditating and would like to change it, then take your awareness to the back of your head behind your third eye and focus. Ask your angels for assistance. (This process is similar to removing cords.) Take your awareness to the root chakra and think of the energy pattern that you'd like to correct from a past life experience. As you clear the past life experience, you are also clearing the karma because that's what it is—reoccurring energy from Earth Mind. Ask the angels to remove it and replace it with unconditional love. This technique seems to help some people; I hope it helps you.

Here is a detailed explanation of the technique I use for clearing past lives:

The first step is to clear the chakras. Next, I take my awareness to Earth Mind. I also contact my angels and guardians. If I am helping someone clear their past lives, I like to have that person physically in the same room with me. Sometimes I like to ask them questions about their behavior patterns and families while I'm working on them. I also like to journal their past life events because this helps the person understand later on what caused their karma in the first place.

After I have prepared myself in a meditative state, I project my awareness to the heart chakra of the person I'm working on and follow their energy down to the root chakra, clearing as much harmful energy out of their chakras as I can. I pull my awareness back even farther and dowse any past lives. I ask if there are past lives that need to be cleared in the last one hundred years, then I go by one-hundred-year periods as far back as necessary.

When I discover a lifetime that needs to be worked with, I ask for details such as the time period it occurred and geographical area in the world (such as Europe, North America, Africa, etc.). Then I narrow it down to a specific location. I find out if they were male or female, their age, marital status, and occupation or means of subsistence. I then isolate the experience to find the lesson to be learned. I am shown a scene of what happened and how the karma was created.

Since the person I'm with has given me permission, I change the situation. I manifest a new intent and replace the standing waves of energy that are holding the situation. I project a new beneficial situation into the zero point of the present. The old form is now changed and no longer exists, and the new situation is projected forward in time up to the present. When I'm done, I remove my awareness from the person I've been working on. I come back into my heart chakra and go up to the third eye and forward to my eyes. I open my eyes and push the other person's energy out of my aura, then I ground myself and make sure I am clear of that energy.

Summary

- Our low soul/self is influenced by our past life experiences. The lessons that we need to experience on our evolutionary journey will continue to manifest with patterns or types of behavior until we recognize and master them.
- Karma is the reoccurring energy from an experience that is either beneficial or harmful to us or others. The goal is to eliminate past karma that has created disturbing challenges for us in our lives so that we can have fulfilling and abundant lives.
- Techniques are available to clear past lives and karmic flow.

CHAPTER 23

RELIGION VERSUS SPIRITUALITY

This is a good time to discuss the difference between religion and spirituality. To be considered religious is simply following the doctrines, tenants, and rules set by the church in order to be in good standing with God and the church. The church sets the standards and you are expected to follow them and not to question them. If you question them, then you may be asked or told to leave, or you may leave and find a similar church that suits your understanding. There are religious people who are very spiritual and have chosen to maintain their religious practices and find it beneficial for their souls. There is no right or wrong choice to make. Many people think that religious practices make them spiritual. In actuality, it does not.

Being spiritual involves our spirit and souls living in the light of the Prime Creator. When we are connected with the Prime Creator, we will manifest the frequency of love from our beings. Our focus will primarily be on expressing ourselves with unconditional love for humankind, and not as much on religious practices dictated by man. We do not need religious involvement or approval to be connected to the Prime Creator. We do not have to join something to be spiritual.

Learning the laws of the universe and practicing the law of love can be a good guide to start with since the purpose is for the benefit of everyone on the earth as well as the universe as a whole. The more we release and replace old harmful energy (which is why clearing techniques are provided in this book) with new energy and unconditional love from the Prime Creator, the more spiritual we become.

The commandment that Jesus gave, noted in the Holy Bible in Mark 12:31—"Love your neighbor as yourself"—can be achieved. This will require you to clear old harmful energy such as malice, hatred, bitterness, jealousy, and resentment from your chakras and fill them with the unconditional frequency of love from the Prime Creator.

Summary

- Being religious means to follow doctrines, tenants, and rules set by a religious group to be in good standing with them and God. Religion expects your obedience. Religious practices do not make a person spiritual.
- It is possible to be religious without being spiritual, spiritual without being religious, or spiritual and religious.
- Being spiritual means to involve our spirit and souls and live in the light of the Prime Creator. Spirituality involves expressing ourselves with unconditional love. The more we learn to clear harmful or unbeneficial thought patterns from ourselves, the more spiritual we become.

CONCLUSION

I hope many of you are able to gain something beneficial by reading this book. Perhaps you're able to achieve clarity in some area of your lives and use your power to change. As each of us awakens to the understanding that we are powerful spiritual beings, we can change our world to become a better place. It starts with one person at a time, living in harmony with oneself and others. If each of us learns to live in accordance with the universal law of love, through the law of oneness, we can unite our separate powers into a collective field of consciousness that will manifest positive changes for our world.

The change begins with each of us learning to live in accordance with the universal law of love and unite our separate powers together. I envision in the future that the principles of the universal laws, explained in this book and taught by many others, will be common knowledge. They will be taught in our educational systems, which will adopt methods and techniques to teach the workings of subtle energy and the universal laws. The result of this will be that generations to come can empower themselves and live in peace and harmony.

Glossary

Affirmations: Declared statements frequently used to manifest. One must use desire, will, and intent combined in an affirmative statement.

Akashic records: The standing waves of energy that hold the sum total of past and present activities of our souls' experience held within the electromagnetic field of Earth Mind.

Angels: Evolved spiritual beings that assist us when we call upon them.

Anointed: The "anointing" experience is a euphoric sensation that occurs when chakras are stimulated by surrounding energy from others; often misinterpreted as the Holy Spirit.

Ascended masters: Souls of former humans who have evolved to a very high state of consciousness. They often work with the angels and aid humans for healing and information.

Astral planes: Fourth and higher dimensions.

Aura: The energy field that surrounds the body. It is comprised of the chakras of the body.

Being: A composite of energy sustaining itself with a consciousness of its own.

Binding: The concept that a proclamation or declared statement remains within a person as well as connected energy fields.

Bonded/cords of attachment: An exchange of energy from one person to another through an energy cord of attachment (an energy link). We can also have cords attached from places and things.

Chakra: The human body consists of subtle energy fields that regulate positive and negative energy polarities. (See chapters 3 and 4.)

Chakra system: The energy centers of the body that vibrate at different frequencies. Each chakra is associated with different levels of consciousness. (See chapters 3 and 4.)

Cocreator: Using our desire, will, and intent to manifest something with the aid of Spirit Source.

Collective consciousness: When a group of people gather and agree on an idea or concept, their energy manifests itself into what is referred to as consciousness (ability an energy pattern has to hold a form of memory within itself). When the energy of this consciousness is collected in a group setting, it is called group consciousness or collective consciousness.

Consciousness: A form of memory holding an energy pattern (i.e., standing waves).

Cords of attachment/bonded: See *bonded*.

Desire: A thought or impulse to create or manifest something.

Devas: This refers to nature spirits which are elemental and intelligent energy forms sent from the Spirit Source that help hold nature in balance and help with its evolutionary process.

Devic spirits: Energy forms from Spirit Source that aid and maintain earth's balance.

Dimension: A field of energy comprised of vibrations of frequencies referred to as octaves. Each dimension is composed of twelve octaves.

Divine consciousness: The universal field of subtle energy that accumulates and holds information and can be used to oversee and aid the universe, earth, and our lives. (This is referred to by some as the *infinite mind.*)

Dowsing: Using a pendulum or device that connects with the subconscious mind and various energy fields to gather information.

Earth Mind: The crystalline field of consciousness located in the earth that holds its own chakra system of consciousness. Referred to as Mother Earth, or Gaia.

Ego: Our individual identity; the middle self expressing itself in balance with the low and high selves.

Energy: The infinite power source from the Prime Creator that is the creative substance of the universe.

Entity/spirit: An energy form that manifests a consciousness and has the ability to perform certain activities. These terms are used interchangeably; however, spirits and entities originate from various places.

Essence: The substance of matter having a consciousness of its own and expressing itself in a specific manner. The distinguishing characteristic of a matter that helps us identify it.

Evolution: The ability given by Prime Creator that allows us to experience all things possible. This is done in a progressive manner that allows us to raise our vibration level.

Free will: Humankind's freedom to express itself as we choose, allowing the spirit and souls to experience all things possible.

Frequency: A waveform of subtle energy.

Gaia: See *Earth Mind.*

God: See *Prime Creator.*

Godliness: A religious term that denotes living by the principles of God.

Group consciousness: See *collective consciousness.*

Growth: The expansion of oneself. It can occur on the physical, emotional, or spiritual level.

Guardians: Beings of extreme intelligence that have evolved over millions of years that work in conjunction with Spirit Source to aid mankind.

Guides: Souls that have previously lived on earth and have chosen to help humans instead of reincarnating. They operate in the fourth and fifth dimensions.

Hell: The negative reality expressed in a discarnate form, usually in a collective field of consciousness.

High self: The high vibration of our chakra system that is our connection with the Spirit Source.

High soul: The intelligence of humans that evolves and carries forward from one incarnation to the next. It is connected to Spirit Source.

I AM: The highest level of oneself in the chakra system that identifies with the Spirit Source.

Incarnation: The evolutionary process in which the spirit expresses itself in a physical manifestation.

Indwelling spirit: A spark of light connected to Spirit Source, located behind our heart. It connects us with energy for our existence and is the center of our essence of being.

Instinct: These are patterns of consciousness drawn from genetic heritage to aid the species in its evolution.

Intent: Knowing and believing that desire and will are manifesting. It is the assurance that what we are manifesting is already complete.

Karma: The reoccurring energy from an experience that is either beneficial or harmful to us or others. Documented in our akashic records. A result of the law of cause and effect.

Kundalini: An energy flow; negative chi energy ascending from Earth Mind through the chakra system, splitting above our heads to descend around the perimeter of the aura, in addition to descending positive energy from Spirit Source that flows through our chakras and splits below the root chakra to ascend in the front and back of the aura. This flow repeats many times. This process clears old and harmful energy from the chakras and energizes the body.

Light: The positive energy of the Spirit Source that is empowering to our chakras. This is the opposite of darkness or negative energy.

Loosing: The concept of releasing undesirable intent, beliefs or energy, such as a bound proclamation or declared statement.

Love: It is the vibration frequency from the Prime Creator with the intent to harmonize and hold the universe in coherence. It expresses itself in the characteristics of giving, sharing, empowerment, and creativity.

Low self: The energy of our primitive consciousness, connected to the low soul. The energy generated in the region of the root and sacral chakras.

Low soul: The human consciousness of our being that is reincarnated and connected to Earth Mind and akashic records; comprised of root, sacral, knee, ankle, and Earth Mind chakras.

Manifest: Using desire, will, and intent to create.

Meditate: Meditation is listening (gathering information) and manifesting desire, will, and intent.

Middle self: The middle self is connected to our ego and self-identity. This is where we manifest things such as love and hate. It is considered the referee or the conscience between the high and low selves and dictates correct or incorrect choices. It keeps us balanced and helps us choose from right and wrong but can be involved in correct or incorrect choices.

Octave: A level of vibratory frequency in a dimension.

Oversoul: The center of our highest awareness. This secondary chakra works with the crown chakra to help us function as a spiritual being; manifests our personality, reality, and personal expression.

Past lives: Previous lives spent on earth.

Polarity: Positive and negative energy expressions in balance. It is also demonstrated in a balance of male and female expression.

Power: Unlimited potential expression to manifest something demonstrated by desire, intent, and will.

Prayer: Making a request and/or expressing thanks to Spirit Source.

Prime Creator: The creator of all things. (See chapter 1.)

Reality: Truth perceived by the observer.

Reincarnation: The cycle of passing from one physical plane to the spiritual plane and repeating the process over and over in the process of evolutionary growth.

Religious: To follow doctrines, tenants, and rules set by a religious group to be in good standing with them and God. Religion expects your obedience. Religious practices do not make a person spiritual.

Self-realization: When we awaken to our inner selves and understand our personal potential.

Soul: The consciousness that holds and carries forward the memory of human experience. It remains after death and continues in reincarnation. (See chapter 7.)

Soul group: A soul group consists of approximately one thousand souls that decide to help one another from life to life. They change roles throughout lifetimes.

Spirit/entity: An energy form that manifests a consciousness and has the ability to perform certain activities. These terms are used interchangeably; however, spirits and entities originate from various places.

Spirit Source: Specific subtle energy connected from Prime Creator to our spirits and souls. It is aiding energy for our souls and spirituality, as well as our connection with the Prime Creator. This energy can be from, but not limited to, spiritual beings such as angels, guardians, ascended masters, and other spiritual beings.

Spiritual: To involve our spirit and soul and live in the light of Spirit Source. Spirituality involves expressing ourselves through unconditional love.

Standing waves: Energy vibrations of frequency that hold a form that can manifest through intent.

Subconscious mind: The total of our memories and information stored in the consciousness of all our chakras.

Subtle energy: From the Prime Creator; substance of all that exists; fundamental to spirituality, energy, and the purpose of our lives. It has no boundaries and consists of positive and negative polarity. (See chapter 1.)

Third eye: Psychic avenue by which spirits are recognized by sight (clairvoyance), sound (clairaudience), feeling (clairsentience), or a combination of the three.

Unconditional love: The concept of love that Jesus taught—also known as the law of love—that allows all things and life forms to exist in harmony.

Universal consciousness: This intelligence of the Prime Creator is referred to as universal consciousness. The universal consciousness maintains balance by established universal laws (something that is constant and doesn't change), which allows it to operate within certain parameters.

Universal laws: Law of love, law of divine oneness, law of attraction, law of polarity, law of vibration, law of cause and effect, law of relativity, law of action, law of compensation, law of correspondence, law of rhythm, law of relativity, and law of gender. (See chapter 2.)

Universe: All existing matter and space considered as a whole; the cosmos.

Vortex: A funnel of energy that connects one dimension to the next.

Will: The agreement to take action on our desires.

Zero point: Referred to as the energy center of the heart chakra, where standing waves are manifested by merging negative and positive energy.

About the Author

Rich Ralston is a clairvoyant energy worker and healer. His abilities include chakra clearing and energy release instruction, past life karma clearing, communication with souls of the dead as well as crossing them over, and remote healing (helping others throughout the world), and much more. He does this to help others heal and learn so they may empower themselves and reach a higher potential. He draws from his past religious experiences to help others gain clarity and perhaps new direction in their lives.

His current project involves communicating with souls of the dead and exploring the realms of afterlife with hopes to share his gained knowledge with others. Feel free to contact him at Subtleenergy101@gmail.com.